THE MARKET STRUCTURE OF SPORTS

△ THE

△ MARKET

▼ STRUCTURE

▼ OF SPORTS,

▼

GERALD W. SCULLY

The University of Chicago Press
Chicago and London

Gerald W. Scully is professor of economics at the University
of Texas, Dallas, and the author of *The Business of Major
League Baseball,* also published by the University of Chicago Press.

The University of Chicago Press, Chicago 60637
The University of Chicago Press, Ltd., London
© 1995 by The University of Chicago
All rights reserved. Published 1995
Printed in the United States of America
03 02 01 00 99 98 97 96 95   1 2 3 4 5
ISBN: 0-226-74394-2   (cloth)
        0-226-74395-0   (paper)

Library of Congress Cataloging-in-Publication Data

Scully, Gerald W.
    The market structure of sports / Gerald W. Scully.
        p.   cm.
    Includes index.
    1. Sports—Economic aspects—United States.   2. Sports
administration—United States.   2. Sports—United States—Marketing.
GV716.S38   1995
338.4'3—dc20   94-16219
                                                  CIP

⊗ The paper used in this publication meets the
minimum requirements of the American National Standard
for Information Sciences—Permanence of Paper for
Printed Library Materials, ANSI Z39.48-1984.

△

△

△ **C O N T E N T S**

▼

▼

△

△

△ **P A R T O N E**

▼ Introduction

▼

▼

△

△

▼   The Economics of Sports Leagues

▼

Introduction

A financial golden age in professional sports has existed for the last
fifteen years or so. Club revenues and player salaries have skyrock-
eted. Attendance is up by 85 percent in baseball, 130 percent in
basketball, and 40 percent in football and hockey. Many clubs con-
tinually sell out. The value of broadcast rights has grown even faster
than attendance: a fourteenfold increase in baseball, a sixteenfold
increase in football, and a seventeenfold increase in basketball since
the mid-1970s. Rapid revenue growth has contributed to about a
tenfold increase in franchise prices since the mid-1970s, with baseball and football franchises selling for about $125 million, and bas-
ketball franchises for $70 million or so. Rapid revenue growth has
fostered aggressive bidding for free agents: average player salary
has risen twentyfold in baseball and tenfold in basketball. As a class,
professional athletes in team sports are among the most highly paid
in society.

But the rose is fading. The prospects for robust revenue and
salary growth in the 1990s have dimmed. Attendance may rise somewhat, but with so many sellouts, its growth rate will decline. Luxury
boxes will be added, and ticket prices increased, but revenue growth
from these and other fan-related expenditures is marginal. The fact
is that ticket prices are set so as to maximize gate receipts. Except
for championship clubs, ticket prices tend to rise at about the infla-
tion rate. The prospects for rapid growth in broadcast revenue are
not promising. Network audience shares have declined drastically

3

(about 50 percent, today), depressing advertising revenues. The networks are less than enthusiastic about bidding aggressively for sports-broadcasting rights. The conventional wisdom is that the value of the national broadcast rights might fall. It is certain that the value of these rights will not grow by much. Some leagues have sought joint production with network television, where leagues and television share risk and profits from televised games. Pay-for-view of play-off and championship games may eventually come for the leagues. While this is technologically feasible (about three-fourths of households are connected to cable), early trials (e.g., the Olympics, boxing matches) have not been promising. Each league is waiting for the other to make the plunge. Through the grace of Congress (the Sports Broadcasting Act of 1961), leagues are allowed to collude in the sale of broadcast rights, but that antitrust exemption can be revoked. Wide media coverage of sports and viewer resistance may make it politically difficult for the leagues to exploit the opportunity of pay-for-view. Thus the era of 20–25 percent annual growth in revenue is over for a time; revenue is likely to grow at about half that rate for the rest of the 1990s.

Club costs have been rising more rapidly than revenue in recent years. With the rapid rise in player salaries, the player share of revenues has been climbing. There is no hard evidence that the player share has reached an upper bound, despite owner complaints (perennial in baseball) that there is not much more room for growth of average player salaries beyond revenue growth. The implication of the rhetoric is that the bidding for free agents will be less aggressive in baseball and basketball. There is some evidence for this view. While baseball-player salaries have risen about 20 percent per year since free agency, the increase was only 2.8 percent in 1993.[1] Now that football has veteran free agency, player salaries have risen steeply, and it is likely that they will converge toward those in baseball and basketball.[2]

The purpose of this chapter is to provide an introductory overview of the economics of sports leagues, both in a historical and current context. Sports leagues are unique in the range of anticompetitive practices tolerated in both the product and players' market. While the degree of anticompetitiveness in these markets has been attenuated over the years, the practices have not been eliminated. Owners have always claimed that restrictions on competition were necessary for the protection of their investments and for competitive balance on the playing field. Are these claims valid or disingenuous?

Economic Structure of Leagues in the Early Period

Baseball

In its early form baseball drew its inspiration from English rounders and cricket. It was first played in America in the later half of the eighteenth century.[3] The game was adopted by amateur athletic clubs, which were social associations of men of means. The first known game that had a playing field and a set of playing rules more or less recognizable today was held at the Elysian Fields in Hoboken, New Jersey, in June of 1846 (New York Knickerbockers versus New York Base Ball Club). The playing field was diamond-shaped, bases were ninety feet apart, nine men were on each team, three strikes meant the batter was out, and three outs retired the team for the inning (the competing field design at the time was the Massachusetts version of a square field with a sixty-foot baseline). Twenty-one aces, or runs, were required for victory. This scoring requirement led to long games, some of which lasted a day and a half. Prior to 1846, teams played with various numbers of players and with rules that suited the occasion.

Amateur clubs dominated the game from its founding until after the Civil War, but barnstorming teams came to town on occasion, and these players were paid. For example, in 1867 the Washington Nationals came to Cincinnati and trounced the local team. In 1869 the Cincinnati Royal Stockings were formed, with Harry Wright as a paid manager. They traveled extensively, won fifty-six games, and had one tie game. The Cincinnati players were paid. Travel of clubs up and down the coast and to the midwest was facilitated by the rise of the railroad. Newspapers, anxious to increase circulation, covered games, and coverage became more extensive as the popularity of the sport spread. Thus the early and mutually advantageous association (circulation for the newspapers and free advertising for the sport) between sport and the media was established. By 1858 the National Association of Base Ball Players (NABBP) was formed—an association of amateur players, not clubs. The association adopted the New York Knickerbocker playing rules, but in the interest of speeding up the games it replaced the scoring rule that required twenty-one aces for a win with a seven- and then a nine-inning rule. Only the leisure class could stay away from work long enough to play or watch such interminable games. The switch to nine-inning games speeded up play and made mass attendance possible. The change in the scoring rule was value-maximizing; it is difficult to believe that baseball would have been commercially viable without such a change.

By 1860 there were players from sixty clubs in the association; by 1867 there were players from three hundred clubs. It is important to recognize that this large number of clubs drew fans from a population that was one-seventh of its current level and in cities that were small by today's standard. There were only 14 cities with populations over one hundred thousand (compared to 186 today), and none with a population of one million or more (today there are seven).

As baseball became more popular, the practice of using paid players in amateur clubs spread, and tension arose between clubs that were strictly amateur and clubs that had paid players. The NABBP tried to impose and enforce standards of amateurism on the sport (membership fees, hearings on infractions, fines, blackballing, suspension), but those clubs that had incentives to pay players maneuvered around the payment ban. A common ruse was to give a player a sinecure in some business of a principal sponsor of the club. Later, as teams began to charge admission to the games, players demanded a share of the receipts. By 1870 the abuse of using paid players was sufficiently widespread to precipitate a walkout of the amateurs at the association's annual meeting. On St. Patrick's Day in 1871, the National Association of Professional Base Ball Players was formed, and that was the beginning of the end of amateur baseball. The association was controlled by the players and lasted for five years.

Until the formation of the National League, the baseball market was competitive. Because entry and operating costs were low, clubs were formed easily. Without entry barriers, there was no restriction on output (number of clubs). There were no restrictions on the input market either—players were free agents. The practice of charging admission (generally ten cents) that was made possible by the game's growing popularity spread with the need to defray player expenses. The commercialization of baseball brought fiduciary obligations as well as profit opportunities to clubs. When Harry Wright demonstrated that commercial opportunities were possible with a roster of paid players, other entrepreneurs followed suit.

The National Association of Professional Base Ball Players was the first professional league. It was an open league—all that was required for membership was the payment of a ten-dollar entry fee. The clubs were financed by investors, but the league was controlled by the players. Payment to the players was the first obligation of a club. Interclub competition for free-agent players, the absence of a fixed playing schedule, gambling, thrown games, player and fan rowdyism, and poor attendance led to financial pressure on the investors. Club turnover was high, disputes over player contract jumping, the playing schedule, ticket pricing, and the gate split were widespread, and the league lacked competitive balance (Boston won four of the five pennants).

In 1876 Chicago promoter William A. Hubert formed the National League, which was an association of clubs. To induce a degree of financial stability, membership was restricted to eight clubs, and franchises were awarded only to well-financed investors in cities with a minimum population of seventy-five thousand.[4] The effect of the minimum-population rule seems innocuous today, because there are more than three hundred such cities, but it was very restrictive at the time. Its effect was to confine baseball to a maximum of two dozen cities. Each club had a monopoly right to its territory. The effect of this rule was to create a wide variance in the financial ability of clubs to compete on the playing field. New York City had a population above one million, and Chicago was growing rapidly, but cities like Hartford, Louisville, Cincinnati, Providence, Indianapolis, Milwaukee, Syracuse, and Troy were small. A fixed playing schedule of sixty games was in effect for the 1877 season. Players were free agents until 1879, but were bound to honor their contracts for the season. To reduce rowdyism, players were subject to a disciplinary code, and liquor sales, gamblers, and Sunday games were banned.

Commercialization changed the character of the game. Increasing revenue and constraining cost became paramount considerations. Fans respond to winners and exciting contests, so winning at any cost became a chief objective of the players. If amateur baseball was gentlemanly, commercial baseball was crude and unsportsmanlike. Play was aggressive and tricky. If an infield fly ball was purposely dropped with a man on base, a double play was made. A runner who interfered with a ground ball could prevent a double play. Much of the expansion of playing rules was intended to keep players from cheating at the margin. While it is now more subtle, such cheating continues to this day (e.g., corked bats, spitballs, scuffed balls). The other motive for expanding the rules was the innovative play introduced by the players. Instead of standing on the bag to field, as they did in the earlier years, they began to position themselves on the diamond for best advantage. Runners, who used to stand near the bag, began to take leads, and they learned to slide to avoid a tag. Pitchers shifted from the stiff-armed underhand throw to an overhand delivery, and they developed change-ups and the curve ball. Players began to specialize in fielding positions; catchers began to wear masks ("bird cages"); fielders began to use leather gloves, at first unpadded, then padded. Many of these innovations led to further changes in the playing rules. For example, with the pitcher's mound forty-five feet from the plate, a ball lobbed underhanded was an easy target (strikeouts were rare). An overhand delivery from forty-five feet came like a rocket to a hitter. Hence, placing the pitcher's mound sixty feet from the plate (the originally intended distance, although it was institutionalized in 1893 at sixty feet, six inches because of a mistake in measurement) made more sense. Naturally, changes in the playing rules altered the defensive and offensive balance within and among clubs.[5]

The idea behind the formation of the National League was to raise the caliber of the game by confining the league to an elite set of teams that had exclusive territorial rights. Baseball at other levels competed with the National League for fans. From 1877 to 1879 the National League faced competition from the International Association. The expectation was that the National League eventually would monopolize the sport, but the early years were financially rough for the league. The disparity in club playing strengths was extreme, and that disparity affected the financial bottom line. The most successful clubs of the period were the Chicago White Stockings and the Boston Red Stockings. The *Note and Account Books* of Harry Wright give the receipts, operating profits, and net worth of the Boston Red Stockings from 1873 to 1882.[6] Total revenue to the club from 1874 to 1882 was $272,339, and total profit was $17,423. Operating profit as a percent of operating revenue was 6.4 percent. The net worth of the club was said to be $767.93 in 1873 and $4,003.95 in 1882. The average annual compound growth rate of net worth (a measure of the value of the franchise) was 20.1

percent. The returns to franchise ownership are operating profits and capital appreciation, so the total returns were 26.5 percent per year.

It is not known whether Wright's estimate of the net worth of the club in 1882 is accurate. James Quirk and Rodney Fort provide information on franchise sale prices for five clubs in the period 1885–1887.[7] Detroit bought the Buffalo team in 1886 for $7,000 to acquire four players. Cleveland was sold in 1885 for $2,500 and was moved to St. Louis. The National League bought Kansas City in 1887 for $6,000. Boston bought the Providence club for $6,600 in 1885, and St. Louis was bought by the National League for $12,000 in 1887. The average sale price of these franchises was $6,800, but none of these clubs were successful franchises.

Most of the National League clubs lost money in the early years, and many of them folded. Some clubs were thrown out of the league (Philadelphia and New York at the end of the initial season for failing to play their quota of games; Louisville for throwing games in 1877; Cincinnati for Sunday games and liquor sales at the end of the 1880 season), and others folded for financial reasons. Table 1.1 illustrates the instability of the league and the disparity of play during its early years. Of the original clubs, only Chicago and Boston survived. Measured over the longer period from 1876 to 1900, when the National League faced competition from other leagues, the failure rate of the franchises seems high. Of the twenty-nine clubs created by the National League or absorbed from the American Association, twenty-one were canceled—a business failure rate of 72 percent over the period. On an annual basis, however, about one club failed per year, a business failure rate of about 3 percent per year. In modern times a similar percentage of small businesses fail each year.[8] Baseball was a new business enterprise, and as such its franchise failure rate seems no more (and probably a good deal less) than would be encountered in other businesses. To claim that entry restrictions and exclusive territory were necessary for financial survival is by analogy to contend that any competitive business—from grocery stores to gasoline stations—needs such anticompetitive practices to survive. There is nothing particularly unique about professional sports that justifies such practices.

Part of the financial pressure on the clubs was player salary levels. At several hundred dollars for a rookie to about three thousand dollars for a star, players were paid several times a working man's

Table 1.1 Early History of Clubs in the National League

Club	Record
1876 Season	
Chicago	.788
St. Louis	.703
Hartford	.691
Boston	.557
Louisville	.455
New York*	.375
Philadelphia*	.237
Cincinnati	.138
1877 Season	
Boston	.700
Louisville*	.583
Hartford*	.534
St. Louis*	.467
Chicago	.441
Cincinnati	.263
1878 Season	
Boston	.683
Cincinnati	.617
Providence	.550
Chicago	.500
Indianapolis*	.400
Milwaukee*	.250
1879 Season	
Providence*	.702
Boston	.643
Buffalo* (1885)	.590
Chicago	.582
Cincinnati** (1881)	.538
Cleveland* (1884)	.329
Syracuse*	.314
Troy* (1882)	.253

*Team ceased to exist.

**Expelled for Sunday games and sale of beer.

wage. Player salary was about two-thirds of a club's costs.[9] Another part of the problem was ticket pricing and the gate split between the home and visiting teams. Dime baseball was the rule prior to the formation of the National League. A ticket price of fifty cents became constitutionally mandated for the National League clubs in 1880. Some clubs in smaller markets objected that the general admission price was too high. Nevertheless, the league-mandated ticket price was enforced. In contrast the rival American Association, which was formed in 1882, charged twenty-five cents admission. An outlay of $2.50 for a day at a National League park was a little steep for a working man's family. High ticket prices contributed to low attendance, and the season was lengthened to offset the effect of the high ticket price. By 1879 the league had an 84-game schedule, and by 1889 a 140-game schedule was in place. Under the mandated gate-sharing arrangement, the visiting club received fifteen cents (a 30-percent share) of the fifty-cent general admission price. Revenue from more expensive seating went to the home club and was justified as an incentive for them to improve their stadiums or to build new ones. Prior to World War II, club ownership of the park was the rule. Clubs in small markets suffered from the gate-sharing arrangement, a problem that has continued in baseball (as well as basketball and hockey, where the visitor gets nothing) but has been alleviated by the rise of large national television contracts that are evenly split among the clubs. Over time, the home-visitor gate split became more extreme. The visitor gate split was down to 14 percent in 1950.[10]

Efforts to control salaries grew more intense as clubs buckled under financial pressure. Owners believed that unrestricted competition for free-agent players was ruining them financially. The first restriction was to ban contract jumping during the season. Although a player was free to negotiate with another club at any time, he was not eligible to play for another team until the following season. In 1879 a reserve rule was introduced. The possibility of player reservation arose because of the collapse of the rival International Association. In that year a club could protect five players, obviously its quality veterans. Clubs typically had about a dozen players, so the reserve rule initially protected about 40 percent of the player roster. The reserve rule adversely affected the high-paid veteran players: either they played for the team that reserved them, or they did not play baseball in the National League. Thus, downward pressure on their salaries began. The profitable idea of league collusion in the players' market was extended. By 1883 eleven men (essentially the whole roster) were reserved, and the league agreed to reciprocally honor player contracts (a nontampering agreement) of the American Association. As roster sizes grew slightly in 1886 and 1887, the number of reserved players expanded.

Player reservation produced the intended consequence, but led to player unionization. Average player salaries fell by about 20 percent between 1878 and 1880.[11] Baseball became profitable as attendance increased and costs declined, but the owners were not satisfied. Further collusion yielded a Limit Agreement in 1885 that set a maximum salary of $2,000 for a player. The players were livid. John Montgomery Ward formed a players' union among the Giants' players that quickly spread to other clubs. Ward was taken in by the owners, however, and agreed that the reserve clause was necessary for the financial stability of the clubs. Player reservation—essentially an indefinite property right in the player's service that was exclusive to the club holding the contract—was written into the Uniform Player's Contract in 1887. For ninety years thereafter, players were reserved by their clubs.

The player-reservation rule eliminated the competitive market for players' services. In addition to suppressing salaries, player reservation created a valuable property right for clubs—the outright sale of player contracts to other clubs for cash. For example, at the end of the 1886 season, right-fielder Mike "King" Kelley was sold to Boston for $10,000. Frequent sales of player contracts by financially weak small-city clubs to big-city teams undermined any competitive balance brought by the player-reservation rule. Player sales for cash were common until after World War II. The innovation of professional sports as a tax shelter in the early 1950s reduced the practice for fear of tax consequences. Player trades became more common, but there was no formal ban on cash sales. The egregious abuse of sales for cash in the mid-1970s by Charles Finley prompted Commissioner Bowie Kuhn to put a stop to it.

Still the owners were not satisfied. In 1888 they advanced the Brush Classification Plan, whereby players would be paid according to skill and skill category—much like a union pay scale. This type of scheme has also appeared in modern times (under Ed Garvey the

National Football League Players' Association tried to get the players and owners to agree to a fixed player share of league revenue and a position and seniority pay scale), but Ward and the players were not enthusiastic. Ward got nowhere in negotiations with Al Spalding, and rather than strike he took advantage of financial interests that wanted to establish a rival league. Thus the Players' League, a sort of players' cooperative, was formed in 1889. Competing with the National League and the American Association (1883–1891), the Players' League lasted just one season.

The attempt of the National League to monopolize baseball created a boom-and-bust pattern in baseball that lasted for a quarter of a century. Restricting output and charging high ticket prices created pockets of unsatisfied demand. In 1877 the National League comprised eight clubs. The International Association competed with the National League in 1877 and 1878. With the collapse of the International Association and the introduction of the player-reservation rule, most of the eight National League clubs made profits. Baseball became a prosperous undertaking during the early 1880s. Naturally, profit opportunities induced the entry of a competing league. The American Association offered lower ticket prices, Sunday games, and liquor at the park. With six clubs in the American Association, there were fourteen teams playing major league baseball. A National Agreement was struck between the two leagues in 1883 that included reciprocal honoring of player contracts. By the 1884 season there were thirteen clubs in the American Association, and the Union Association entered as a league, so that a total of thirty-four clubs competed in major league baseball. Table 1.2 shows the distribution of major league clubs by city. New York and Philadelphia had three clubs each. There were seven cities with two clubs, and fourteen other comparatively small cities had major league baseball.

The Union Association collapsed after one season. From 1885 to 1889 there were eight clubs each in the National League and the American Association. In general both leagues did well financially. For example, by 1889 Brooklyn of the American Association, with a pennant-winning 93–44 season, drew over three hundred thousand fans. The Players' League added eight clubs, and with the American Association's nine clubs a total of twenty-five major league clubs competed in the 1890 season. The aftermath of the Players' League was a struggle between the National League and the American Asso-

Table 1.2   Distribution of Major League Clubs by Cities
in the 1884 and 1903 Seasons

City	Clubs in 1884	Clubs in 1903
New York	3	3
Philadelphia	3	2
Baltimore	2	0
Boston	2	2
Chicago	2	2
Cincinnati	2	1
Pittsburgh	2	1
St. Louis	2	2
Washington	2	1
Altoona	1	0
Buffalo	1	0
Cleveland	1	1
Columbus	1	0
Detroit	1	1
Indianapolis	1	0
Kansas City	1	0
Louisville	1	0
Milwaukee	1	0
Providence	1	0
Richmond	1	0
St. Paul	1	0
Toledo	1	0
Wilmington	1	0

Source: *The Baseball Encyclopedia*, 8th ed. (New York: Macmillan, 1990).

ciation over player reassignment. The National Agreement was voided, and the 1891 interleague war contributed to the collapse of the American Association. The National League absorbed four American Association clubs and bought off the others. The National League became a twelve-club league from 1892 to 1899. On the whole, baseball was profitable during the 1890s. By the 1900 season, however, the National League had only eight clubs, and the restricted output induced entry of the American League (Ban Johnson's former Western League) for the 1901 season. Under the 1903 National Agreement, the National League and the American League functioned as separate and equal major leagues. The distribution of major league clubs by city in 1903 is given in table 1.2. Baltimore lost major league baseball, although it had two clubs in 1884. Major league baseball was confined essentially to large urban areas, with only sixteen clubs playing until expansion in 1961.

The National Agreement set the preconditions for financial stability in baseball. Between 1903 and 1920 baseball attendance grew about 50 percent, from about 5,000 per game to about 7,400 (today a typical club draws about 27,000 fans to a game). During the 1920s total baseball attendance remained in the 9–10-million range. Because of the reserve clause, costs rose modestly compared to revenues. In 1920 the average club made about $142,000 in profit.[12] At the end of the decade, average club profits were $84,143 on average revenues of $750,000.[13] Operating profits as a percent of operating revenue averaged 11.2 percent. Within the period there were eight franchise sales. The average franchise appreciation rate was 15.8 percent per year. The total return to franchise ownership in 1929 was about 27 percent per year. These returns are comparable to those earned today (see chapter 6).

Basketball
Basketball appears to have been invented by James Naismith at the International YMCA Training School in Springfield, Massachusetts, in the winter of 1891. Originally played with nine-man teams, peach baskets affixed to the balconies of the gym, and a soccer ball, the game caught on quickly. As it evolved between 1891 and 1900, the rules of play were very fluid. There was no limit to the number of players—Cornell University hosted a game with fifty players on each side. Play was defensive and rough, and twenty-point games were common. The first college game played under rules similar to today's was between Yale and Pennsylvania on March 20, 1897, with Yale winning 32–10. By 1900 the rules of play included five-man teams, two-point field goals, and a one-point foul shot. The game quickly became commercialized, much as baseball did, with barnstorming clubs. After the YMCA discontinued the program as un-Christian, it rented out its scarce gym facilities to promoters who staged games. Frequently the games were packaged with dances and

music to draw customers, and players were paid any residual after rent and the promoter's fee were subtracted. Originally players were hired by the promoter on a per-game basis. Promoters were known to slip out of town with the proceeds, leaving the players unpaid. The first professional league, the National Basketball League, was formed in 1898 among clubs in Philadelphia.

There is very little financial information available for the early period in basketball (as for football and hockey). The paucity of data precludes making an assessment of profitability and capital appreciation rates during the formative years. Nevertheless, the pattern of franchise instability seen in baseball prior to the National Agreement holds in these sports as well.

Basketball leagues were regional until the formation of the American Basketball League (ABL) in 1925. These regional leagues formed and collapsed, and club turnover was high. The ABL lasted until 1931, when it became inactive. It was revived in 1933 as a regional league. The National Basketball League (NBL) was formed with thirteen clubs in 1937. Five clubs folded in 1938, and by 1942 the league was down to four clubs. The NBL expanded to a dozen clubs after World War II, but faced competition from the eleven-club Basketball Association of America (BAA) (the American Basketball League operated after World War II, but merged with the BAA). The National Basketball Association (NBA) was formed in 1949 out of the ashes of the financial ruin of the NBL and the BAA. Originally composed of seventeen clubs, the league had shrunk to eight by 1954. From 1946 to 1959, fourteen franchises were abandoned in the NBA (inclusive of the BAA).[14]

The period from 1946–47 to 1948–49 in the NBL and the BAA affected the shape of the NBA in its initial season. The NBL located franchises in areas where amateur basketball was popular and where most of the players (who were white) originated. As table 1.3 shows, most of these clubs were in relatively small towns. The BAA adopted a big-city strategy. As clubs failed after the 1946–47 and 1947–48 seasons, the NBL tended to add clubs in small towns. The BAA tended to move in this direction also by replacing some of its failed clubs in larger cities (e.g., Toronto, Cleveland, Detroit, and Pittsburgh) with franchises in Rochester, Fort Wayne, and Indianapolis. Attendance records for this period are limited to a few of the larger-city clubs in the BAA: per-game attendance at Boston, Philadelphia, and New York was in the 3,500–5,000 range.

Table 1.3   The Distribution of Basketball Club Cities, 1946–64

1946–47	1947–48	1948–49	1949–50	1954–55	1963–64
Rochester	Rochester	Rochester	Rochester	Rochester	
Ft. Wayne	Ft. Wayne	Ft. Wayne	Ft. Wayne	Ft. Wayne	
Toledo	Toledo				
Syracuse	Syracuse	Syracuse	Syracuse	Syracuse	
Tri-Cities	Tri-Cities	Tri-Cities	Tri-Cities		
Youngstown					
Oshkosh	Oshkosh	Oshkosh			
Indianapolis	Indianapolis	Indianapolis	Indianapolis		
Chicago	Chicago	Chicago	Chicago		
Sheboygan	Sheboygan	Sheboygan	Sheboygan		
Anderson	Anderson	Anderson	Anderson		
Detroit		Detroit			Detroit
	Flint				
	Minneapolis	Minneapolis	Minneapolis	Minneapolis	
		Hammond			
		Dayton			
		Waterloo	Waterloo		
		Denver	Denver		
Washington	Washington	Washington	Washington		
Philadelphia	Philadelphia	Philadelphia	Philadelphia	Philadelphia	Philadelphia
New York	New York	New York	New York	New York	New York
Providence	Providence	Providence			
Toronto					
Boston	Boston	Boston	Boston	Boston	Boston
St. Louis	St. Louis	St. Louis	St. Louis		St. Louis
Cleveland					
Pittsburgh					
	Baltimore	Baltimore	Baltimore		Baltimore
				Milwaukee	
					Cincinnati
					San Francisco
					Los Angeles

Source: David S. Neft and Richard M. Cohen, *The Sports Encyclopedia: Pro Basketball,* 3d ed. (New York: St. Martin's Press, 1990).

The initial membership of the NBA was seventeen clubs. Only six of them were located in the ten most populous metropolitan areas. Nine clubs were located in comparatively small population areas. The NBA began to shrink immediately. It had eleven teams in 1950–51, ten in 1951–52, nine in 1953–54, and eight in 1954–55. Franchises were canceled in large and small cities alike. In the 1954–55 season there were three large-city clubs (New York, Philadelphia, and Boston). Fort Wayne, Rochester, and Syracuse were small markets. A big-city strategy began the following year, when the Milwaukee Hawks moved to St. Louis. After the 1956–57 season, the Fort Wayne club moved to Detroit, and the Rochester club moved to Cincinnati. In the early 1960s Minneapolis and Syracuse were replaced by Los Angeles and San Francisco. Chicago and Baltimore (Washington) were added by expansion. By the 1963–64 season, the nine-club league had located in the most populous cities.

Initially, attendance at NBA games probably was not much different from what it had been at the games of the precursor leagues. The earliest league data is for the 1952–53 season. Average home attendance was about 3,200 per game. Boston, Philadelphia, and New York drew more fans (about 3,950 per game), while the smaller-city clubs drew less (about 2,900 per game). By the 1963–64 season, average attendance per game was about 5,000. Most of the increase is due not to the increased popularity of the sport but to the location of the clubs in larger cities. With its location in large metropolitan areas, basketball was transformed into a big-city sport, and integration opened the sport to blacks from large cities, who have come to dominate the game. To place the attendance figures for the period in perspective, current attendance averages over 15,000 per game, and about half of the clubs have sold-out or nearly sold-out seasons.

Football

The origin of football is obscure, but its clearest roots are traced back to rugby, first played at Rugby College, England, in 1823. The game took hold in America among college athletic clubs—naturally in the Ivy League. The playing rules were a mixture of the rules in soccer and in rugby. The first known game was between Princeton and Rutgers in 1869, played on a field measuring 120 by 75 yards, and Rutgers (my alma mater) won, six goals to four. Under the

Princeton rules of play, twenty-five men were on each side; eleven-man teams did not appear until 1880. The rule of ten yards in four downs did not appear until 1912. By 1876 the playing rules were those of rugby. By today's standards, scoring was peculiar. A safety was one point, a touchdown was two points, an after-touchdown conversion was four points, and a field goal was five points. A field goal of three points and a touchdown of six points were not introduced until 1910 and 1912, respectively. The game as played by the college boys was very rough, and injury was frequent. In 1905 this led to the formation of the Intercollegiate Athletic Association, the precursor of the NCAA.

Professional football took much longer to appear than professional basketball. While it was played professionally as early as 1895 in Pennsylvania, professional football did not catch on. In 1920 the American Professional Football Association was organized by George Halas and owners of other professional clubs in the Midwest. A franchise cost $25. The initial pattern of franchise location, franchise mortality, and low attendance in football was similar to that of the early years of baseball and basketball. The National Football League that was established in 1922 grew out of the American Professional Football Association. Table 1.4 gives the locations of professional football clubs that operated from 1920 to 1929; note that few clubs were located in large metropolitan centers. Attendance at games was low (about 3,600–5,000 during the 1922–24 seasons),[15] comparable to that at NBA games in the early period. College games, particularly at the major football schools, outdrew professional games by a large factor and continued to do so for several decades. Clubs located in the larger cities outdrew their small-city rivals by a factor of two or three to one. During the period from 1920 to 1929, twenty-nine franchises folded.[16] The shift to a big-city strategy is seen in table 1.4. By 1960, with the rise of the American Football League, the vast majority of clubs were located in or near major population centers. Attendance per game averaged about 23,000 in 1960. This strategy was maintained after the AFL-NFL merger in 1970; by then, attendance per game was about 50,000.

Restrictions in League Product Markets in the Modern Period

All professional sports leagues restrict entry, assign exclusive franchise territory, and collude on a revenue-sharing formula. In general,

Table 1.4   The Distribution of Football Club Cities,
             1920–70

1920–29	1960	1970
Akron		
Boston	Boston	Boston
Buffalo	Buffalo	Buffalo
Canton		
Chicago	Chicago	Chicago
Cincinnati		Cincinnati
Cleveland	Cleveland	Cleveland
Columbus		
Dayton		
Decatur		
Detroit	Detroit	Detroit
Duluth		
Green Bay	Green Bay	Green Bay
Hammond		
Hartford		
Kansas City		Kansas City
Kenosha		
Louisville		
Marion		
Milwaukee		
Minneapolis		Minneapolis
Muncie		
New York	New York	New York
Orange		
Portsmouth		
Pottsville		
Providence		
Racine		
Rochester		
Rock Island		
St. Louis	St. Louis	St. Louis
Tonawanda		
Washington	Washington	Washington
	Philadelphia	Philadelphia
	Pittsburgh	Pittsburgh

Table 1.4   (*continued*)

1920–29	1960	1970
	San Francisco	San Francisco
	Baltimore	Baltimore
	Los Angeles	Los Angeles
	Dallas	Dallas
	Houston	Houston
	Oakland	Oakland
	Denver	Denver
		Atlanta
		New Orleans
		Miami
		San Diego

Sources: *Official 1985 National Football League Record and Fact Book* (St. Louis: The Sporting News, 1986); David S. Neft and Richard M. Cohen, *The Sports Encyclopedia: Pro Football*, 8th ed. (New York: St. Martin's Press, 1990).

Note: Green Bay games were played in Milwaukee.

public policy tolerates this collusion. Baseball is formerly exempt from the antitrust statutes since a unanimous court in *Federal Baseball v. National League et al.* [259 U.S. 200 (1922)] ruled that baseball was not engaged in interstate commerce and was therefore exempt from the antitrust statutes. The legal standing of collusion in baseball has been reaffirmed in several decisions since then. The other team sports do not enjoy formal exemption except in two important matters. When a collective bargaining agreement exists or remains in force despite a labor dispute, player-league disputes are exempt from antitrust under the labor exemption. Second, in 1961 Congress passed the Sports Broadcasting Act (amended in 1966), which extends the antitrust exemption to the negotiation of the sale of league broadcasting rights. Thus the league packaging of broadcast rights for sale to the broadcast networks is perfectly legal.

Team sports are naturally collusive at some minimal level. A game or a contest is a joint output. To produce it, the teams must agree on a set of rules governing the contest and on the division of revenues. All sports began with barnstorming clubs. Some clubs emphasized entertainment, and frequently contests with the locals were mismatches. The Harlem Globetrotters are the only remaining club with a barnstorming tradition. The limited commercial appeal of a single contest or a series of contests between the same two teams led to the rise of groups of teams formed as leagues. A league is the natural unit of economic organization. While still having entertainment value, league play is different. A club's financial bottom line depends on its performance against clubs of similar quality over a season. Sports fans appear most interested in organized championships with a high caliber of play among the contestants.

Leagues establish constitutional agreements governing the geographical markets of their franchises, conditions of entry and franchise relocation, the market for players, and playing regulations. These agreements, or league operating rules, tend to be privately joint-wealth maximizing[17] and collusive. While barriers to entry in the Stigerlian sense exist in other industries (e.g., gate space in the airline industry, shelf space in supermarkets), permission of the current firms in the industry is not a condition of entry for new firms.[18] In order for new teams to enter a league or for existing franchises to relocate, permission of the existing members must be secured.[19] The Oakland Raiders moved to Los Angeles in 1982, and the Clippers moved from San Diego to Los Angeles in 1984 without league permission. The Raiders won the antitrust suit with the NFL, the Clippers paid $6 million to the NBA for invading the Lakers' territory. Since these unilateral moves, the ability of leagues to legally enforce territorial restrictions is ambiguous, but leagues still exercise considerable monopoly power in the geographical markets in which contents are held.

Leagues provide contests with a degree of uncertainty of outcome. A set of rules governing the contest must be formulated and followed by the teams to insure the ordered outcome of the games. These consist of uniform rules of play, scoring, scheduling of games, use of equipment, and so on. Without such rules, disputes about the outcomes of games would be widespread, and championships would be suspect. Teams must therefore collude to some degree, if only to establish uniform playing rules and establish a credible champion.[20] If all teams within a league were of equal playing strength, the schedule of contests would not be relevant to the establishment of a champion. When wide variation exists in team quality within a sport, league organization and scheduling ensure that each competitor engages a similar number of teams in a similar number of contests.

League rules that define membership, conditions of entry, division of territorial rights, and division of revenues from contests are not necessary for the provision of games but exist in the interest of rent-seeking. Owners have argued that these collusive agreements are justified to protect franchise values. While such rules are wealth-maximizing for the existing club owners, they are unique in American business. Under common law such cartel agreements are not enforceable, nor is competition recognized as a tort. Thus a dry cleaner on a particular city block has no standing in a court of law for recovery of lost value of his assets when a competitor locates next door. Second, even though the price of an existing franchise might be as high as $250 million, the purchase consists largely of player contracts and the right to be the exclusive provider of games in a geographical market, not meaningful physical assets.

A more compelling economic argument for these restrictions on the number of clubs and for exclusive territory is that in their absence the quality of team contests would be lower. Quality of play in team sports has two dimensions: absolute and relative. The absolute quality of play is its level, and that depends on the quality of athletic talent fielded. While minor league baseball, college baseball, football, and basketball, and the various amateur leagues may be exciting in their own right, the absolute quality of play is lower. If the supply of high-quality playing talent were perfectly elastic, the number of major leagues or teams within a league would have no effect on the absolute quality of play. But prime athletic talent is scarce. The huge differential in player pay versus the player's next best occupational wage is evidence of the low elasticity of supply of prime athletic talent. Because the addition of teams to a league dilutes the quality of play by spreading a more or less fixed supply of star players over a greater number of teams, restrictions on the number of teams increase the absolute quality of play.[21] Similarly, the rise of a competing league reduces the absolute quality of play. From the perspective of the fans, some restructions on the number of leagues in a sport and teams within a league may be socially desirable.

In the course of time, leagues have expanded. Until 1962 baseball had eight teams in each league; in the 1993 season there were twenty-eight clubs. In 1951 football consisted of two conferences, each with six teams. Now there are twenty-eight teams, and expansion is under consideration. In the 1954–55 season basketball consisted of eight teams in two divisions; now there are twenty-seven teams. Further domestic expansion of the various leagues, while contemplated (e.g., in football and hockey), will be difficult for several reasons. The remaining potential sites tend to be in small population centers or in larger metropolitan areas that already have clubs. The expansion fees are very high, mainly to cover the present value of reduced national broadcast revenues. The prospect for robust growth in revenues is dim, and with free agency in baseball, basketball, and now football, an investor can no longer get into a sport cheaply.

These leagues have not expanded because of a desire to supply contests in a market previously not served, but to preempt entry by a new league.[22] If, say, eight teams is the minimum size for a league, sufficient population growth in eight other locations that would financially support a league brings the threat of the formation of a rival.[23] New leagues are not signatory to existing league cartel agreements. Players precluded from moving to teams within leagues can gain financially by jumping to the new league. Of course with veteran free agency in three of the sports, the incentive for jumping to a new league is reduced, but not eliminated. Competition for player talent leads to large increases in average player salaries that threaten the financial stability of the leagues. By expanding judiciously, existing leagues can preclude the entry of a competing league. However, demand is never fully satisfied. It pays leagues to keep several sites open. This induces cities without franchises to compete with cities that have them for an existing franchise. (A recent example was the proposed move of the Giants from San Francisco to St. Petersburg.) Such teams threaten to move or do relocate to acquire new stadium facilities or other benefits on more favorable terms. One consequence of this behavior by leagues is that 87 percent of the stadiums and 65 percent of the arenas are publicly owned, and rent of the facilities is heavily subsidized by taxpayers.

The second dimension of playing quality is relative. Relative playing quality is measured by the dispersion in team standings. A distribution of team standings in which team A always beat team B, team B always beat team C, and so on would yield a very large variance in team standing. Such games would not be contests, but exhibitions, and there would be little fan interest in the games of such a league. On the other hand, if each team had an equal chance of beating another, then team records would be .500, with a small variance due to random factors. Knowing that it was simply luck or the erroneous decisions of referees and umpires that caused a team to be the champion or the bottom finisher would also reduce fan interest in the contests of such a league. This suggests that there is an optimal degree of uncertainty or variance in team standings that maximizes fan interest, revenue, and profits to the clubs. Fans want their home team to win under uncertainty. Some degree of uncertainty of outcome is a necessary feature of competitive team sports, and this uncertainty is largely determined by the relative playing strengths of the teams within a league. Greater equality of playing strengths and hence more uncertainty about the outcome of games, up to some level, is wealth-maximizing. League attendance and probably Nielsen ratings are higher when team standings are closer within a league over a season.[24]

The relative playing strength of a team depends on the financial strength of the team and the owner. Teams earn revenue from ticket sales, concession income, and the sale of broadcast rights. The main cost for a team is for the player roster. Teams face the same supply function for player services (incremental cost), but different demand functions for games.[25] The restrictive practices of the sports cartels in the product market and the rule on revenue division among the teams in a league have implications for the dispersion of team standings.[26]

Prior to the rise of television, teams earned revenues from ticket sales.[27] Attendance is determined mainly by franchise market size (measured crudely by SMSA population size) and the club win-loss record.[28] Because teams are located in cities of markedly different sizes, the ability to field a competitive team is affected by franchise market size and the cartel rule on the division of the gate receipts. Consider the extreme cases. In basketball and hockey the home team gets all of the gate receipts, the visitor gets nothing. In 1990–91 the top revenue-producing basketball club had 3.5 times the revenues of the lowest revenue-producing club. In baseball the overall gate split is 85–15. The top club had 2.5 times the revenues of the weakest club in 1990–91. In football the gate division is 60–40.

The top club had 50 percent more revenue than the lowest club. Obviously, given the unequal size of cities, the more unequal the division of the gate receipts, the more unequal the division of revenues among the clubs within a league.

The long-run, steady-state win percent of a club is that record that maximizes profit.[29] Technically, this is a condition where incremental revenue from wins equals the incremental cost of producing that win record. Because population size differs among clubs, assuming that the fans' demand for wins is geographically invariant, average and incremental revenue differ by a scalar among the clubs. Teams in cities with large populations have maximum profits with records above .500; teams in cities with small populations have maximum profits with records below .500. It is no accident that large-city teams historically have dominated as championship teams, particularly in baseball (e.g., the Yankees, with thirty-three championship titles) and basketball (e.g., the Celtics, with sixteen titles).

The Cartelization of Broadcast Rights

In the early years broadcast rights were negotiated locally. Most clubs simply sold their rights to a station that packaged the games. Some clubs purchased air time and put the games on themselves. In a few instances clubs sold their rights to sponsors who put the games on the air. In all instances restrictions were placed on the use of the rights. By reciprocal agreement among the clubs, broadcasts to the home market were blacked out when the team was playing at home; only away games were broadcast. In 1946 the major leagues adopted a rule preventing the broadcast of other clubs' games into the home territory when games of the club were at home. Clearly, this practice was anticompetitive. Under pressure from the Justice Department, the leagues modified the rule in 1950. While a number of anticompetitive practices arose in the 1950s, the fact that several networks or stations competed among themselves and with a large number of providers of broadcast rights had implications for the distribution of rents between clubs and television. When there were three baseball clubs in New York, three network stations, and several independent stations, a fair semblance of competition existed in the market for broadcast rights.

The first league-wide packaging of rights was between the National Basketball Association and NBC-TV in 1954. Baseball followed suit with "Game of the Week." In 1960 the American Football League pooled its rights and sold them to ABC. The NFL and CBS had a similar agreement in 1961. By pooling broadcast rights, the leagues eliminated interclub competition in their sale and increased their share of the rents relative to the networks' share. The ban on the broadcast of home games remained. Leagues shopped the networks for the best deal, and because broadcast rights are very valuable, each network increased its offer in each successive round of negotiation. While one network emerged a winner by locking up the broadcasts of a particular sport for a few years, the other networks were unsatisfied and a potential source of trouble if a rival league emerged. Recall that ABC had AFL games while CBS had NFL games. One could argue that the survival of the AFL as a league was made possible by access to national television, which helped financially in its own right and brought recognition and fan interest.

The courts vacated the CBS-NFL contract, and the status of pooled broadcast rights was in doubt throughout sports [*U.S. v. National Football League,* 116 F. Supp. 310 (1953), 196 F. Supp. 445 (1961)]. What the courts undid, however, Congress permitted. On September 30, 1961, Congress passed the Sports Broadcasting Act, which permitted leagues to act as cartels in the negotiation and sale of their broadcast rights, and to be free of any antitrust sanction. The league sale of rights to a specific network for a specific period of time continued, but the NFL later moved to an arrangement in which all of the networks got some of the games, some of the time. The great advantage of this arrangement was that all of the networks had an interest only in NFL games. There was no unsatisfied demand that a potential rival league could exploit to improve its chances of surviving.

From the point of view of the fans, who are interested in the chances of their local team having a winning season, the various arrangements in the sale of broadcast rights have had both positive and negative consequences. When broadcast rights were sold on a club-by-club basis, the fans got to see their local team's away games, but not much else. Because the value of local broadcast rights is a function of broadcast market size, big-city clubs obtain much more revenue than small-city clubs. Television increased the dispersion in club revenues, and to the extent that financial inequality promotes inequality on the playing field, it increased further the gap between wins and losses among clubs. Local rights remain an important source of variation in club revenues in baseball and basketball.[30]

With the rise of national rights and league pooling of these rights, fans see a wider array of games, but unless the local club is sold out, they do not see home games. Now that there are three networks and a few national cable networks, fans can view a fairly large number of games, but not all of them. Cartels restrict output to raise the value of the product. Hence the current arrangement means that a substantial number of fans cannot view the games in which they have a particular interest. On the other hand national television contracts have grown in importance as a source of revenues to clubs in all professional team sports, and these revenues are divided equally among the clubs. As these evenly divided revenues have grown as a fraction of total club revenues, the dispersion in club financial strength has narrowed. More equality of revenue has led to more equality of play. While the dominance of big-city clubs has not been eliminated, it has been attenuated.

There are two important, interconnected antitrust issues in professional team sports. First, entry restriction and exclusive territory preclude a larger number of clubs except by voluntary expansion, so that expansion will at best be limited. Second, the collusive arrangement between the existing leagues and television largely precludes the formation of rival leagues.

Because of the Sports Broadcasting Act, the cartel arrangement in the sale of broadcast rights acts as a powerful barrier to the entry of a potential rival league. Sports programming is extremely valued by the television networks. The demographic profile of viewers is attractive to a certain class of advertisers, whose willingness to pay some of the highest advertising fees in the industry has propelled the growth of network television revenues to the leagues. By allocating games to all three networks, the NFL has co-opted the networks as a partner in the enterprise. Further, the contract stipulates that other professional football games cannot be broadcast by the networks within forty-eight hours of an NFL game. This relegates any competing league's games to mid-week, which is hardly attractive to the networks.

Television appears to increase the demand for attendance at games, and thus indirectly increases gate receipts.[31] Certainly the effect of television is to build team recognition and loyalty among fans. The USFL was formed as a competing league, and part of the reason for its failure may be its inability to secure broadcast contracts sufficiently lucrative to compete on an equal financial footing with the NFL.

Access to television may be a necessary condition for the survival of a new league. The NFL has an exclusive multiyear contract with the networks. Only at the time of that contract's expiration is there a possible point of entry, but that implies that the networks would find the games of a new league to be suitable substitutes for NFL games. New leagues are inferior to established leagues in the quality of play (consider the quality of the games of the World League, an NFL creation manned with players who could not make an NFL club), and it takes many seasons of play for them to achieve parity. It is entirely possible that the viewing audience would be smaller for the games of a competing league, giving the networks little incentive to substitute the games of a new league for NFL games.

Technological change in the broadcast industry potentially reduces the barrier to entry. The Fox and Paramount networks are seeking to compete head-on with the older national networks. To do so they need original programming. There are many cities in the United States with independent VHF stations. Location of franchises in these VHF cities and a broadcast contract with Fox (Paramount) might create the necessary conditions for the survival of a new football league. The decline in audience share of the three national television networks has reduced their financial resources sufficiently to make a new league's arrangement with Fox or Paramount financially attractive. Yet under the broadcast exemption there is nothing to prevent the NFL from selling some games to Fox or Paramount; the revenue would be less than with the networks, but the NFL could thereby preclude entry of a new league.

Largely at the urging of Senator Connie Mack (R-FL) who was upset with the way baseball treated the investors who had hoped to bring the Giants to St. Petersburg, Congress once again held hearings on baseball's antitrust exemption. The hearings were notable only for the sympathy expressed for Fay Vincent. All senators favored removing the exemption, but would it really matter for baseball? After all, the other team sports are not exempt and appear to be doing better financially. If more product competition is desirable as a matter of public policy, it is the revocation of the Sports Broadcasting Act that would make it possible for rival leagues to enter the various sports. Let us suppose that this happened.

If entry was unrestricted in sports, what would the sports markets look like? Would this be in the interest of fans, club owners, and players? Under a completely free market, it is possible that clubs in the existing leagues might relocate to larger metropolitan markets (e.g., more clubs in New York, Los Angeles, Chicago) and that new leagues would be formed. Many cities without clubs might have them. In the interest of self-preservation, such clubs would probably sort themselves out into regional leagues that contained clubs of more or less comparable quality, as in collegiate sports. Let me continue to speculate on a structure that might be attractive to sports fans. Pennant winners in such regional leagues could engage in a series of play-offs with each other, as divisional winners currently do in the existing leagues. A World Series or Championship Series would follow from these play-offs. Thus, in principle, a world-champion club could be established in sports organized in a free market. With complete freedom of competition, including the market for players' services, no club would dominate for long in a sport.

As the fan base was spread over a larger number of teams, however, revenues would fall, and the value of the existing franchises would plummet. Salaries would fall as club revenue fell, while Joe Montana, Patrick Ewing, or Roger Clemens might be among the best players, they certainly would not be paid four or five million dollars. On average, players' pay would be more comparable to the average pay in the economy; their opportunity cost. Premier players would earn a premium, as high achievers do elsewhere in the economy, but a star would earn only a few times, not fifty times, what a rookie earned. Players in professional clubs therefore have as much at stake in maintaining the anticompetitive restrictions of the existing leagues as do the owners.

Would a free market in professional sports benefit fans? That is hard to say. If absolute quality of play means more to them than having a hometown club, fans would suffer. Clearly the absolute quality of play would decline. Say that one hundred of the regular roster players in baseball are the stars. These players would be spread over many more teams. On the other hand, if having a local club means more than restricted access to high-quality clubs, fans would benefit.

The fact that so many rival leagues in professional team sports have failed can be interpreted as evidence that absolute quality of play matters to fans (and that relative quality of play matters also, since competitive balance frequently was absent). On the other hand the American League and the American Football League were successful entrants, and the American Basketball Association was partly successful. Most observers have judged that the absolute quality of play was inferior to the NL, NFL, and NBA. Moreover, a number of minor league baseball clubs (e.g., Louisville) draw a million fans or so, and with about a hundred schools competing in Division I-A college football, and more in basketball, attendance is large and enthusiastic. Nearly forty million fans attend college football games, with schools like Michigan drawing one hundred thousand fans or more per game. We do not know what trade-off fans would make between absolute quality of play and an expansion in the number of clubs. Certainly the existing size of the big leagues is not a reflection of that trade-off. League expansion is governed by the constraint of not adversely affecting current franchise values. Only a free market (free entry and exit by clubs) in professional team sports would tell us the fans' preferred trade-off between absolute quality of play and the number of professional clubs.

The Players' Market

Historically, teams were invested with exclusive bargaining rights with the players. All of the leagues established collusive agreements that governed the selection, contractual arrangements (exclusive contracts with the signing club, which then owned the rights to the player's services), and distribution of players among the clubs. Collectively these powers granted a great degree of monopsony power to the clubs in the various sports. Monopsonistic exploitation (pay less than a player's incremental contribution to club revenue) of baseball players was in effect from 1879 to 1976, in basketball until the mid-1970s, and in football until recently. The only other important example of monopsony was in the market for actors and actresses in motion pictures.[32]

Substantial reforms in the market for players have improved player-initiated movement among teams, but by no means is there an open and competitive market for player services. Rather, an elaborate set of rules determines which teams can negotiate with which players for their services. These agreements also are collusive and anticompetitive.

Athletes enter professional sports through a drafting procedure. The various types of drafts are intended to distribute the rights to the acquisition of amateur players to the professional clubs. The common feature of the drafts is that they grant to the team exclusive bargaining rights for the services of the prospective player. Once drafted, the athlete negotiates with that team. While these rules have been weakened somewhat over the years, they still impede aggressive bidding for amateur players. Once a player has come to terms with the drafting team, he must sign a standard players' contract. The contract restricts the sale of his services to the team holding the contract (until death in baseball during the era of the reserve clause, and for a fixed length of time today). While there are variations in these contracts from sport to sport, which will be discussed below, all contain some basic prohibitions restricting player-initiated mobility. The rules for player transfer are more favorable to the players in baseball, basketball, and (beginning in 1993) football than in hockey.

There are considerable differences in the average pay and in the distribution of pay between players in the various sports. The differences are correlated with the degree of restrictiveness of player-initiated mobility, the nature of the production function in the sport, and the arrangement for dividing the revenues among the teams. When the players' market was very restricted, players made somewhat more than the average American worker, and salaries were more or less equal across team sports. In 1967 the median family income of Americans was about $8,500, while players in baseball, basketball, and hockey on average made about $20,000. Football players made about $25,000.[33] With veteran free agency and the tremendous growth of revenues in sport, mainly due to television, players now make from seven to thirty times the median family income of Americans. Baseball and basketball have the highest average salaries—a little over $1 million in 1992. In football, Plan-B free agency (the system ended in 1992) increased average player salary. On average, NFL football players made about $500,000 in 1992. Hockey players are subject to the greatest restrictions in the players' market. While Wayne Gretzky made $2.7 million with the Los Angeles Kings, the average hockey player earned about

$350,000 in 1992. As of 1992, salary differentials were less wide in football and hockey.

At current salary levels, a superstar baseball or basketball player makes up to fifty times the salary of a rookie player. Certainly it is not true that a superstar player is fifty times as productive as a rookie player. The economic justification for a fairly wide salary differential in professional sports is as an incentive to induce all players to perform at their maximum level. Rather than monitor player performance, although this is easier in sports than in other occupations, players signal their own quality. In essence they are offered a two-part contract. One part is payment for expected performance. The other part is a prize: the probability of becoming a superstar and earning the salary and perquisites of stardom. The probability is endogenously determined by the player's performance. Thus the high pay of superstars arises less from owner altruism than from the fact that it shifts the cost of ensuring player performance at maximum levels to the players themselves. These issues are analyzed in chapters 2 and 3.

The relatively high starting salary of rookie players (e.g., $100,000 in baseball) is also economically rational. Certainly the average salary of a player's next best alternative occupation is a fraction of the rookie salary. But the probability of making a professional team is small. Hence rookie salaries times the probability of making a team (expected salary) must exceed average nonsport salaries to insure an adequate pool of athletic talent.

Owners have always claimed that restrictions on player movement were necessary to maintain competitive balance and to protect franchise values. Economists have always been skeptical of the motives and of the evidence.[34] Economists and owners always agreed that there would be a tendency for star players to wind up on big-city teams, but restrictions on player-initiated movement have no bearing on the distribution of playing talent within a league. If players are free to move between teams, holding preferences for location constant, they will tend to play for the team that pays the most. Obviously there are exceptions. Apparently Dennis Eckersley accepted a lower salary to stay with the Oakland Athletics than he could have gotten by moving to another club. The team that will pay the most is the one that expects the largest increment in revenue from that player's service. Because an increment in the win record brings more fans into the stadium or arena in New York than in Kansas City, the very best players tend to go to the big-city teams. In a market where players are not free to move, does a small-city team that acquired a star player in the amateur draft keep him? In Kansas City or Seattle, say, the team holding the contract expects the player to contribute $1 million in incremental revenue to the club. In New York or Los Angeles that same player would contribute $3 million. Absent a league ban on player sales for cash, the small-city franchise will have an incentive to sell the player's contract to the big-city team and capture some portion of the differential rents. Thus players are allocated by highest incremental revenue, with or without restrictions on player-initiated movement. This is not to say that all of the star players wind up on big-city clubs. The marginal revenue product of stars declines with the number of star players on the roster (i.e., a .700 record does not generate that much more attendance than a .600 record). For example, the 1927 Yankees, probably the most dominant baseball team ever assembled, had a .714 win percent. The "murderers row" of Ruth (60 home runs), Gehrig (47 home runs), Meusel (103 RBIs), and Combs (a .356 batting average) drew a crowd of 1,164,017. The 1926 championship team, with a record of .590, drew only 91,885 fewer fans. While these restrictions have little implication for the allocation of player talent within a league, they dramatically affect the division of rents between owners and players. Under free agency, the players receive most of the rents arising from their scarce talent; under league restrictions on player-initiated transfers, the owners get most of the rents.[35]

Restrictions on player movement have been reduced because of the rise of aggressive leadership in the players' associations. Before the arrival of Marvin Miller, the Major League Baseball Players' Association was a captive of the owners. Eschewing union militancy and standard practice learned with the steelworkers, Miller sought to rally players around issues of common interest (minimum salaries, Murphy money, pension benefits). Seeking consensus among the players and reaching near unanimity among them, Miller then negotiated with the owners, confident of player backing. His strategy strengthened his hand in negotiation, and it was based on an important insight into player behavior. A player's career is short—about five to seven years (less in football). Any gains made through strikes by the union are at the potential expense of the current players and for the benefit of rookies and future players. Because few of the gains can be capitalized (pensions are an exception), players have relatively weak incentives to strike, or to stay out on strike for a long period. This is perhaps the main reason for the long period of time that elapsed before players and their unions became militant in sports.

After their victory in *Curt Flood v. Bowie Kuhn* [407 U.S. 258 (1971)], the owners were in a charitable mood. They offered, and the players' union accepted, final-offer arbitration to settle pay disputes in an "equitable" fashion. That mechanism led to the demise of the reserve clause for veteran players, a story too well known to repeat. Now veteran players are eligible for free agency after six seasons, and players with three years' experience are eligible for arbitration. The rise of free agency and arbitration partly explains the dramatic increase in player salaries from an average of $46,000 in 1975 to slightly more than $1 million in 1992. All is not fair in the player-owner salary game, however. There is evidence of owner collusion in the free-agent market in the mid-1980s.[36] Average player salaries had been rising 26.6 percent per year between 1980 and 1983, rose at an average rate of 12.2 percent during 1984–86, and actually fell by 2.1 percent in 1987.[37] The owners are also very much opposed to the arbitration scheme as it is currently structured. The nearly 50-percent increase in average player salaries in the 1991 season and the 20-percent increase in the 1992 season have brought management-player tension to the forefront once again. The players' association wants free agency extended to players with fewer than six years' experience. The owners want a team salary cap, as in basketball. The players want more extensive revenue sharing among the clubs, a proposal favored by the small-city teams. At this writing, the dispute seems to be less about a new structure governing the allocation of players among the clubs than about the terms, and the parties are far apart.

Larry Fleischer was also aggressive and successful in loosening the restrictions on player-initiated movement in basketball. Despite the fact that clubs paid 70 percent or so of their revenue in salaries and benefits, numerous court cases were filed by the players during the mid-1970s [e.g., *Robertson v. NBA*, 389 F. Supp. 867 (S.D.N.Y., 1975), aff'd 556 F. 2d 682 (2d Cir. 1977)] in an attempt to break the restriction on player mobility (an option/compensation system) and the amateur player draft (a selected player had to sign his first contract with the club that selected him or the team designated by the selecting team). These cases were used to block the merger of the NBA and the ABA. Between 1977 and 1981 players gained some mobility. Prior to the mid-1970s the compensation was sufficiently high that aggressive bidding for players was limited. The agreement with the players' union that allowed the merger liberalized the rules on interteam competition for veteran players and for rookies. The option clause was removed, and compensation was reduced and then eliminated in 1980. It was replaced by a "right of first refusal," under which a club may match the offer of a competing club and keep the player. While the amateur draft was retained, rookies were permitted free agency if they did not sign with the drafting team within two years. Although this was an improvement, a two-year hiatus in the beginning of a professional career that lasts on the order of five to seven years was a pretty stiff tax on amateur players.

Full free agency was not achieved until 1983. In that year the NBA adopted the salary cap as well as a salary floor. The minimum guarantees that about 53 percent of league revenues are to be paid in player salaries. In theory, teams can pay players as they please, subject to an overall limitation on team salary. In the 1987 round of negotiations, the union pushed for the elimination of salary caps, the right of first refusal, and the player draft. Failing to reach agreement, the union sued the NBA under antitrust, and in 1988 threatened to decertify as the collective bargaining agent for the players (such a procedure is necessary for standing in an antitrust suit). The owners and the players settled with complete free agency after four years or the expiration of the second contract (whichever is shorter), the retention of the team salary cap, but the elimination of the right of first refusal. Additionally, the rookie draft was reduced to three rounds, with an eventual reduction to two rounds. The concession on the amateur draft is less favorable to rookies than it would appear. While later-round draft choices do make professional clubs, the first two rounds (about 50 or so amateur players) contain the best prospects.

Player-owner relations have been poorest in football. Ed Garvey ran the NFL Players' Association more as a union than as an association of individual players with some common interests, and his successor, Gene Upshaw, is perhaps more militant. Strikes and confrontations with little or no gains for the players had been a historical feature of player-management relations. Until recent times, in theory, players could play out their option year and become free agents. But a team signing a free agent was subject to a compensation requirement. The "Rozelle Rule," which was in effect until the Mackey case [*Mackey v. NFL,* 543 F. 2d 606 (1976)], had such a high compensation requirement (generally two first-round draft choices) that player-initiated movement was virtually precluded. Since then, and until recently, the compensation formula was related to the quality of the veteran player being signed, with half of those players valued at one or more first-round draft picks. In the 1987 round of collective bargaining, the union demanded unrestricted free agency for four-year veterans and free agency subject to a right of first refusal for players with less than four years of service. The owners refused, insisting on the compensation requirement. No agreement was reached between the parties. The players had been without a collective bargaining contract since 1987. The union strategy was to win free agency in the courts. With a raft of player-initiated antitrust suits against the NFL and a trend in findings for the players, the owners returned to the collective bargaining table, and finally agreed to veteran free agency in 1993.

On March 1, 1993, a new owner-union agreement went into effect that covers the period 1993–99. Players with five years of service are eligible free agents, provided their contracts have expired (initially about 360 players were in this category). The Washington Redskins had the most eligible players (26) and New England (5), Pittsburgh (5), and the championship Dallas Cowboys (6) the least. The free-agency signing period is approximately March 1 to July 15 of each year. Under the so-called Rooney Rule, the top-finishing clubs are prevented from going into the free-agent market unless they have lost a free agent. Then they may bid up to the salary of the player lost. These restrictions only apply in years when there is no salary cap. If player salary costs reach 67 percent of designated league revenues, a salary cap is imposed, and eligibility for free agency becomes four years rather than five. The salary cap begins at 64 percent for 1993 then declines eventually to 62 percent for the remaining period of the contract. A salary floor of 58 percent of designated revenues (about 95 percent of league gross revenues) is imposed. In 1992 player salaries were about 57 percent of designated revenues. An important point for the owners is that one "franchise" player is reserved, but his contract must equal or exceed the average of the top five salaries in that position of 120 percent of his prior year's salary, whichever is greater. For 1993 two free agents per club (designated as transition players) are subject to the right of first refusal, so long as they are offered a contract that equals or exceeds the average of the top ten salaries in that position (or 120 percent of the prior year's salary). NFL clubs were required to designate their franchise and transition players by February 25, 1993. While nearly all clubs designated their quota of transition players, only ten designated a franchise player. Apparently many owners did not believe that important players on their clubs were worth the price of the designation. For example, Jim Harbaugh made $1.35 million with the Bears in 1992. If he had been designated as the franchise player, his 1993 salary would have had to rise to $3.3 million. If he had been designated as a transition player, his salary would have had to increase to $2.9 million. He was designated as neither, but the strategy did not work; the Bears negotiated a $13 million, four-year contract with him. On the other hand Steve Young earned $2.5 million in 1992 with the 49ers. As the designated franchise player for 1993, his salary must rise at least $800,000. With the ending of Montana's career in San Francisco and Young's credible performance, the designation makes sense for the 49ers. The relatively low demand for franchise-player designation by clubs is due to the wide disparity in positional player pay. As veteran free agency increases player salary, these pay anomalies will tend to be reduced. It is likely that more players will be designated as franchise players in future years.

In 1994 the right of first refusal drops to one player. The annual college draft is reduced from twelve to seven rounds, and those clubs losing the most free agents are to be granted extra selections. The salaries of rookie players are constrained to $2 million per club, but allowed to grow if revenues increase. On the whole, rookie players and amateurs got little from the agreement. Collectively, the restrictions on drafting amateur players and the rookie salary cap will make bidding for their services less than aggressive. Finally, owners collectively had to make a $195 million payment to settle all outstanding litigation with the players who had sought free agency in the courts.

While five-year (potentially four-year) veterans have free agency, and marginal rookies made some gains (those drafted after the seventh round), to a lesser degree players with three or four years in the NFL were helped by the agreement. A club must offer $275,000 or 110 percent of the prior year's salary, whichever is greater, to have a right of first refusal on a three-year veteran. For four-year veterans, the offer must be $325,000 or 110 percent. If the club does not match the offer, it is entitled to a draft pick equal to the player's original draft round. Clubs can receive greater compensation by making higher salary offers. If a club offers $600,000 to a three-year veteran (or, $700,000 to a four-year veteran), it will receive a first-round draft choice if the player goes to another club. If the salary offers are $800,000 or $900,000, respectively, the club will receive a first-round and a third-round draft choice if it loses the player.

Restrictions on player mobility are greatest in hockey. Prior to 1974 players were indefinitely reserved by their clubs, as in baseball. In 1974 existing players were free to move between clubs, subject to a compensation requirement set by an arbitrator. Rookie players were subject to reservation for three years. In 1984 the owners imposed a compensation requirement similar to the one that had been in effect in the NFL until recently. The basic structure is in the 1986 union-management collective bargaining contract. Under new directorship, the players' union is showing more militancy. A short strike in the 1992 season threatened the Stanley Cup play-offs. It was settled without much gain for the players.

The agreement between owners and the players' union in football is important as a harbinger of what may come from negotiations in the other sports. The football agreement is notable for its extreme legalistic detail and the substitution of union control over the player's financial destiny for management control. The trend in player-management negotiations in baseball and basketball has been a whittling away of the details in restrictions on veteran free agency. Eligible players negotiate their salaries through agents, not the players' union, as will be the general tendency in football, where stipulations on pay and pay increments have been negotiated between the union and the owners. First, there is likely to be a further expansion of free agency to baseball and basketball players who are not now eligible. With the agreement in football as a model, however, and baseball owners bitter about the explosion of player salary, that trend may be reversed. If such a reversal is to occur, it will appear first in the upcoming player-management negotiations in baseball. The owners want to eliminate salary arbitration, fix player salaries as a share of revenue, and restrict the competition for free agents. The ideas coming from the football agreement, such as a negotiated pattern of salary caps, reservation of a franchise player (subject to pay at least the average of a certain number of comparable players), right of first refusal for one or more veteran players (with certain salary guarantees), compensation for players with fewer than the stipulated number of years for free agency based on the value (pay) of the player, and so on may be attractive to both parties. While the players' representatives now are more like an association representing independent professional contractors, in baseball and basketball they may tend to become more like unions if they follow the path taken by the National Football League Players' Association. The tendency in all labor organizations is for more control over their memberships.

Second, the executive directors of sports unions are suspicious of owner claims of financial distress. The owners in football, by virtue of their settlement, seem to think that they can protect profits and franchise values by agreeing to raise player salary share from its 1992 level of about 54 percent of gross revenues to perhaps 64 percent. For 1992, player salaries as a share of revenues were about 53 percent in basketball and just below 50 percent in baseball. The players' associations in these sports are likely to ask the following question: If football owners believe that they can make a profit with a player salary share that might become perhaps ten points higher than in their sports, why can't baseball and basketball owners do the same? No one knows the steady-state player salary share in the various sports. It is easy enough to state the condition theoretically. The equilibrium salary share is that amount that leaves the owner just willing to stay in the business. The competitive rate of return (profit as a share of operating revenue and capital appreciation of franchises) to franchise ownership might be about 10–15 percent per year, about half of the current rate of return.

PART TWO

The Players' Market

▼   The Structure of Player Salary

▼

Introduction

Under player reservation (perpetual contracts in baseball or option-year contracts with high compensation costs in the other team sports), salary was substantially less than marginal revenue product. Studies on the effect of increased competition in the players' market assert that free agency has aligned salary and marginal revenue product.[1] The implication of this view is that there is a piece-rate, intra-team salary structure within which players who contribute more to team output (revenue) receive proportionately more compensation than players who contribute less.

Casual observation suggests very large changes in salary for very small changes in player share of club output (revenue). For example, Andy Van Slyke made $4.25 million with the Pirates in 1992 and $2.16 million in 1991. Salary is based on past performance, with the most recent season most highly weighed. He played in 136 games in 1990 and 138 in 1991. He had a slugging average of .465 in 1990 and .446 in 1991. Clyde Drexler made $350,000 at Portland in 1987–88 and $1.2 million in 1988–89. The prior seasons saw him play 3,114 and 3,064 minutes respectively and score 1,782 and 1,231 points. Frequently players who are a small fraction better than other players earn several times their salary. The intrateam salary structure definitely is not piece rate, nor has it ever been. The pay structure is hierarchical, as in a rank-order tournament.

In the Becker-Stigler bonding model, life-cycle variations in worker output may induce variations in life-cycle earnings.[2] Edward

Lazear has shown that job monitoring may induce a life-cycle profile similar to the human capital model, with earnings less than the value of the marginal product in the early portion of the career and greater than its value in the later period.[3] Risk-neutral workers presumably are indifferent between a wage profile of spot wage equal to spot value of marginal products at each time period and one of $w < VMP$ initially and $w > VMP$ later on in the life cycle when the present value of the two earnings streams is equal. But employers are not indifferent to the two payment schemes. They prefer a higher level of worker effort to a lower level (shirking). A back-end-loaded compensation schedule induces optimal worker behavior and aligns workers' interests with those of the employer. Lazear and Rosen model the intrafirm salary structure as a rank-order tournament.[4]

In professional sports, team owners or event sponsors want all the competitors to develop their athletic skills to their maximum potential and expend the maximum effort per contest. The desire is profit-motivated: contests among highly skilled contestants who expend the maximum effort at winning are more valuable. This fact implies that there will exist an optimal hierarchy of payments (in team sports, an intrateam salary structure) that aligns player behavior regarding investments in developing playing skills and in expending effort per contest with the owner's objective function. Here the intrateam salary structure is modeled as a team rank-order tournament: competition among players for starting positions that are highly rewarded and backup positions that pay much less. The optimal intrateam salary structure is found for conditions of free agency and player reservation. With a large cross-sectional/time-series sample of baseball and basketball player salaries for the pre- and post-free-agency periods, life-cycle earnings and productivity profiles can be estimated and compared for the first time in the literature.

Team Rank-Order Tournaments and Optimal Intrateam Salary Structure

During the course of a season, a club's performance is determined by the level of talent on its roster and by luck. The probability that one team will defeat another in a randomly scheduled contest is determined by the quality of that team's performance relative to the performance of the opponent.[5]

Clubs derive revenue from two main sources: the sale of broadcast rights in a national market and the sale of local rights (attendance at home games, possibly with a share of the gate to the visiting club, and the sale of local broadcast rights). National rights are evenly split among the clubs in the league without regard to the performance of particular clubs. It is assumed that these shared revenues are determined by league-wide talent levels.[6]

A typical baseball club roster is composed of fifteen players and ten pitchers. Eight of the players are regulars, and usually there will be two backup or bullpen catchers, two utility infielders, and three utility outfielders. Among pitchers, half will be starters, and half will be relievers, who often specialize in middle and closing innings. A typical basketball club roster has a center, two forwards, and two guards as starters, and the backup players are distributed positionally approximately in those proportions. While each position in the various sports is necessary for play, it does not follow that each position produces the same value for a club. For example, if hitting (frequency and bases advanced) is more valued as an attribute of play than other attributes, then on average, outfielders contribute more value than infielders. If the number of points scored is more valued in basketball than other attributes of play, then forwards contribute more value than centers or guards.

Let V_n be the value contributed by play in the nth playing position. Then

$$V_n = \int_0^{t_n^*} [\bar{B}_j' + L_j' f(T_j - T_k)] \, (\partial T/\partial t_n) \, dt_n, \qquad (2.1)$$

where $f = F'$ is the probability density function (pdf) of $(\epsilon_k - \epsilon_j)$ and t_n^* is the optimal player investment in position n, to be defined below. The variables $\bar{B}$, league-wide revenues per club, L, local revenues per club, and T, club playing talent are defined in notes 5 and 6.

Performance in professional sports is related to athletic endowment (exogenous attributes such as reflexes, speed, coordination, agility, height, etc.), intangible attributes of talent (determination, intensity, concentration, and hustle), and player and team investments in enhancing playing skill (training and dietary regimes for increasing strength, endurance, and agility, and practice at hitting, pitching, basket throwing, etc., coaching, and so on). There is little intersport substitution of playing skills; different sports therefore presumably value different athletic attributes, or weigh them differently.

Team members compete for the n positions on a club as starters or backups. While the conventional modeling in a rank-order tournament is of individual sports, where competitors face a fixed prize structure and achieve the next higher reward by advancing one position in the rank of competitors, competition for playing positions in team sports as starters or backups is broadly similar. Starters are always threatened by the performance of the lower-ranked backup players. In a sense the threat of the backup players makes the performance of the starter like a serially repeated contest with competitors. It often happens that as starters experience stochastic or serial patterns in their performance (a slump), backup players are substituted in the lineup. In basketball, for example, in addition to a slump (cold hand in shooting), players tire, are injured, or foul out, and backup players are substituted. A backup player can and sometimes does capture a starting position. In what follows, the two-player rank-order tournament for the nth playing position is serially repeated with random pairings of players in one-on-one contests. As a practical matter, the set of competitors for the playing position may be smaller than in a golf or tennis tournament, but it is by no means trivial. Players face competition from players on the bench, from minor league players, and from players on other clubs who can be traded. In this sense a player in position n on a club is repeatedly playing against all players in that position in the major and minor leagues.

A player's performance in a rank-order tournament for a starting position is determined by his athletic endowment and enhanced by his investment in playing skill, plus exogenous factors that affect performance stochastically (health, weather, playing surface, performance slumps, injury, luck, etc.). The probability that player 1 will defeat player 2 in a random pairing for a contest and obtain the starting position is determined by the quality of player 1's performance relative to that of player 2.[7]

Given an intrateam salary structure that pays S_1 to the starting player and S_2 (with $S_1 > S_2$) to the backup player, the expected earnings of the players are determined by the probability that player

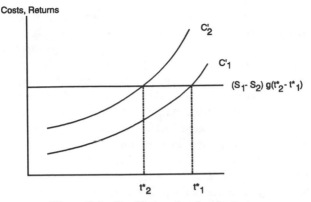

Figure 2.1   Equilibrium levels of talent.

1 beats player 2 for the starting position, p_{12}, and the salary for the two positions (S_1, S_2).[8]

Playing skill is enhanced by player investment at cost $C_i(t_i)$, with the marginal cost of investing rising with the amount of investment $(C_i', C_i'' > 0)$. Because some attributes of playing talent are endowed, $C_i(t_i)$ differs among players. For convenience, let player 1 have a larger endowment of athletic talent, so that his marginal cost of investment in playing skill is lower $(C_1' < C_2')$. Players invest in the development of playing skills to maximize expected net income, $EY_i = ES_i - C_i(t_i)$, which, assuming an interior solution exists, requires that

$$\frac{\partial EY_i}{\partial t_i} = (S_1 - S_2)\, d(t_1 - t_2) - C_i'(t_i) = 0, \qquad (2.2)$$

where $d = D'$ is the pdf of $e_2 - e_1$. The Nash-Cournot assumption is that each player makes investments in enhancing playing skills, assuming that the level of playing performance of the competitor is fixed. If athletic endowments differ among players, which is likely, and if a stable Nash-Cournot equilibrium exists, like the one depicted in figure 2.1, then $t_1^* > t_2^*$ and $p_{12} < 0.5$. Stability requires that $C_1'' > C_2''$ by a sufficiently large amount at the equilibrium talent levels. If the salary differential between the starter and the backup is large, which it is in professional team sports, it is sufficient that C_2' equal C_1' plus a constant, and that C_i', $C_i'' > 0$.

The value of contests to a club, $V = \Sigma_n V_n$, is a positive function of the playing talent on the club. The intrateam salary structure, $S_1 - S_2$, controls investments in playing skills via equation (2.2). Increased player investments add to the value of the club's contests, but S_1 will have an upper bound that is constrained by profits, and S_2 will have a lower bound that is constrained by the opportunity cost of the backup player. For opportunity cost $\bar{C}$, this constraint implies that the lower-bound salary of the backup player in position n is $ES_2 = C_2(t_2^*) + \bar{C}$.

There has been a vast change in the degree of competitiveness in the players' market. Prior to free agency, the players' market was monopsonistic. Under perfect competition in the players' market, $S_1 + S_2 = V_n$ (with $\Sigma_n(S_1 + S_2) = V$). With monopsony power, $S_1 + S_2 < V_n$. That is, $S_1 + S_2 = cV_n$, where $0 < c \leq 1$ is a parameter that reflects the degree of competitiveness in the players' market. Profit and opportunity-cost constraints uniquely determine S_1 and S_2 at each position, as given by

$$S_1 = cV_n\left[\frac{p_{12}}{(2p_{12} - 1)}\right] - \left[\frac{C_2(t_2^*) + \bar{C}}{(2p_{12} - 1)}\right]$$

$$S_2 = \left[\frac{C_2(t_2^*) - \bar{C}}{(2p_{12} - 1)}\right] - cV_n\left[\frac{1 - p_{12}}{(2p_{12} - 1)}\right], \qquad (2.3)$$

with S_2 positive.

There are some interesting implications in equation (2.3). First, the greater the degree of monopsony power (the smaller the value of c), the narrower is the intrateam salary structure ($S_1 - S_2$). While this has consequences for both S_1 and S_2, the lower bound on S_2 is binding. Monopsony power mainly will lower the salary of the starting player, S_1. The greater degree of monopsonistic exploitation of star (starting) players under the reserve clause has been shown before.[9] Second, the monopsony-induced shrinkage in the intrateam salary structure lowers investments in playing skills in general, t_i^*, and investments by players with superior athletic endowments (starters) in particular. That is, $t_1^* - t_2^*$ is greater the higher the value of the competitive parameter, c. This fact has implications for the pattern of playing investments over the career. The levels of investments in playing skill are larger the greater the value of the parameter c, and these investments are sustained for a longer period. These differential investments will take the form not only of increased practice to hone playing skills during the playing season, but the substitution of investment (weight training, conditioning, dietary restrictions, etc.) for leisure and the good life during the off-season. Today few baseball players play with potbellies, as did Babe Ruth, or show up for a game with a hangover, as some did. As a result of this investment pattern, career performance profiles may rise at a steeper rate (reach an earlier peak) and decline more slowly as players age.

Empirical Evidence

Over the years, I have collected data on ball-player salaries from various sources.[10] With a sample of baseball players that spans the years 1964 to 1992 and of basketball players from 1968–69 to 1988–89, it is now possible to estimate life-cycle earnings profiles under conditions of monopsony (prior to 1976 in baseball and prior to 1983 in basketball) and competition in the players' market. In some instances all salary observations for a player are available; for most players there are multiple observations of salary over the career interval.

For baseball players the dividing line between a monopsonistic and a competitive labor market is clearly drawn. In the spring of 1976 a collective bargaining agreement was signed that led to the current system of veteran free agency. In basketball the dividing line between monopsony and competition is less clear. Prior to the formation of the American Basketball Association (1967–68), monopsony prevailed in the National Basketball Association. With the formation of the ABA, players in the NBA had an alternative source of employment. Interleague competition raised player salaries dramatically. However, once signed by a league, players were not free to jump leagues. A number of injunctions were filed by clubs seeking to prevent moves of this sort. By 1973, at least for some star players, the monopsony power of the NBA was weakened. A modest amount of veteran free agency existed after the NBA-ABA merger. On April 1, 1983, the players' union and the owners agreed to a plan of free agency for players, a fixed share of revenues as player salary share, and a system of club salary floors and caps.

Two propositions about player salary are well known: Salary and performance are closely linked, and starting players earn much more than backup players. The link between pay and performance is straightforward in baseball and basketball, because the production function is additively separable (not perfectly so, however), and the player contribution to club performance is readily measured. Club revenues and club victories are highly correlated. The objective of a club is to beat the opponent. In both sports this means scoring more than the opponent. The objective function is to maximize the win percent subject to a profit constraint.[11] This is achieved by maximizing runs or points and minimizing opponent runs or points. In baseball, runs are maximized by obtaining bases or advancing on the bases. A hit, an extra base hit, a walk, and a stolen base all contribute to an increase in runs. Opponent runs (bases advanced) are minimized through pitching and fielding. In basketball, points are maximized through scoring (field goals, free throws). Opportunities for scoring are increased through rebounds and assists. Opponent points are minimized through blocked shots, steals, and rebounds.

While many variables have been specified in prior cross-sectional studies of earnings determination in baseball and basketball, the approach here is parsimonious. For baseball players (hitters) the performance measure is the prior season's total bases (singles + doubles + triples + home runs + walks + stolen bases). Because salary is negotiated prior to the season, last season's performance is appropriate. Salaries rise over time, reach a peak, and then tend to decline toward the end of the career. I can illustrate this pattern in career salary with three ball players for whom I have a complete salary history. The salary histories from 1978 to 1992 (in 1991 dollars) of Gary Carter, Brian Downing, and Alfredo Griffin are shown in figure 2.2. In each case salary declined toward the end of the career. This career salary pattern is partly due to the fact that performance profiles are not flat. Over a certain portion of a player's career, performance tends to improve. The performance pattern is partly due to the hierarchical structure of pay in sports. Incentives to perform and to improve performance that is endogenously determined by player investment and effort increase the probability of obtaining the prize of high pay for being a starting player and for outstanding performance. The conventional method of capturing this aspect of the player performance profile is to use years spent as a

Figure 2.2 Salary histories of three baseball players, 1978–92 (in 1991 dollars).

player or player age (in some studies the square of the variable is included to capture nonlinearity in the earnings profile). Such a variable, however, treats all years as effort-constant. Many players have careers of substantial length during which they play irregularly. To control for player talent, investment, and effort, the career sum (and its square) of games played up to the prior season of the observed salary is utilized here.

In basketball the performance measures are points scored, rebounds, and assists for the prior season. To capture the dimension of the rise of player pay over time and to control for player talent, investment, and effort, the career sum of minutes (and its square) played up to the prior season of the observed salary is utilized. Injury appears to be a more serious problem in basketball than in baseball. In selecting observations, those players with injuries that led to a significant change in their performance records were dropped.

Life-Cycle Earnings Profiles and Freedom of Player Movement
The estimated earnings profiles for baseball players appear in table 2.1, and for basketball players in table 2.2. The samples were col-

Table 2.1 GLS Estimates of Earnings Functions in Baseball

Variable	1964–75		1977–92	
	SALARY$_t$	SALARY$_t$	SALARY$_t$	SALARY$_t$
CONSTANT	10.054	9.931	10.338	10.303
	(179.22)	(166.02)	(131.02)	(125.93)
TOTBASES$_{t-1}$	.173	.181	.283	.305
	(12.47)	(12.99)	(15.31)	(16.20)
SUMGAMES$_{t-1}$	$1.036E-03$	$1.031E-03$	$3.141E-03$	$3.091E-03$
	(14.04)	(14.43)	(32.39)	(32.39)
SUMGAMES**2$_{t-1}$	$-1.728E-07$	$-1.810E-07$	$-9.859E-07$	$-9.771E-07$
	(4.85)	(5.27)	(18.38)	(19.31)
D75		.255		
		(4.05)		
D73		.185		
		(6.21)		
D72		.124		
		(3.49)		
D69		.187		
		(4.98)		
D68		.129		
		(3.27)		
D92				.269
				(7.31)
D89				$-.492$
				(13.69)
D88				$-.209$
				(6.14)
D87				$-.198$
				(5.62)
$\bar{R}^2$	.684	.704	.716	.759
N	895	895	1,895	1,895

Note: SALARY and TOTBASES are in logarithms.

Table 2.2 GLS Estimates of Earnings Functions in Basketball

Variable	1968–75 SALARY$_t$	1984–88 SALARY$_t$
CONSTANT	9.451	9.800
	(35.95)	(43.63)
POINTS$_{t-1}$	.205	.321
	(3.80)	(5.00)
D7375*POINTS$_{t-1}$	.094	
	(13.67)	
SUMMINS$_{t-1}$	3.811E−05	5.106E−05
	(3.58)	(8.15)
SUMMINS**2$_{t-1}$	−6.592E−10	−3.405E−10
	(1.92)	(2.82)
ASSISTS$_{t-1}$	.145	−.103
	(3.40)	(2.66)
REBOUNDS$_{t-1}$		.228
		(5.61)
D88		.146
		(3.69)
$\bar{R}^2$	.643	.630
N	271	479

Note: SALARY and the performance measures are in logarithms.

lected as follows. All baseball players on the 1992 and 1991 rosters were utilized for the period 1977–92. For the 1964–75 period, all of the players appearing on rosters in those years were utilized. All basketball players appearing on the 1988–89 rosters were utilized for the period 1984–85 to 1988–89. For the period 1968–69 to 1975–76, all of the players appearing on rosters in those years were utilized. Obviously, the sample of salary observations is much thinner in times distant, yet the sizes of the samples are substantial. For baseball during 1964–75, $N = 895$, and during 1977–92, $N = 1,895$. For basketball during 1968–75, $N = 271$, and during 1984–88, $N = 479$. Players with less than two years of experience are not included in the samples because most are rookies who earn the league minimum wage. The variance in the performance of these players is great compared to the variance in their earnings. In addition to the performance and career games (minutes) measures, certain dummy variables (e.g., D75) were incorporated. For baseball's monopsony period (1964–75), 1975 was the year in which a significant effect of binding salary arbitration was found. Other years are there because they were statistically significant, mainly because of significant increases in the minimum salary (e.g., a 1969 increase to $10,000 from $6,000). During the free-agency period (1977–), the years of owner collusion in the free-agent market (1987–89) and the extraordinary adjustment to the pent-up demand for free agents in the 1992 season are included as regressors. Other years were insignificant and are the reference dummy. For basketball's quasi-monopsony period (1968–75), there is a slope dummy for the years 1973–75. In this period the strategy of the players' union in blocking the ABA-NBA merger appears to have had its greatest effect in reducing restrictions on player movement. In the free-agency era (1984–), the only dummy that was significant was for the 1988–89 season. All salary observations were deflated by the CPI (1991 = 100).

By White's test, all of the earnings equations exhibited heteroskedasticity. To correct for this problem, all of the earnings functions were estimated by generalized least squares (GLS). The earnings functions in baseball in table 2.1 reveal different coefficient estimates on TOTBASES, SUMGAMES, and SUMGAMES**2 for the monopsony and competitive period. The elasticity of real salary with respect to performance rises from .181 under monopsony to .305 under free agency, an increase of about 70 percent. An F-test on the significance of the difference in the coefficients was significant at well above the .001 percent level ($F = 43.7$).[12] A similarly large difference for the coefficient of salary with respect to SUMGAMES is evident. The coefficient nearly triples in the period of free agency (from $1.036E-03$ to $3.091E-03$). An F-test reveals that the difference is highly significant ($F = 465.9$). The SUMGAMES**2 coefficient also changes significantly (from $-1.810E-07$ to $-9.771E-07$). An F-test on the difference in the coefficients yielded $F = 247.6$. A joint test on the constant terms, the TOTBASES, the SUMGAMES, and the SUMGAMES**2 coefficients was significant ($F = 12{,}002.5$). The $\bar{R}^2$ and the t values of the coefficients reveal that the specification is more than adequate for the purpose at hand.

For basketball, the elasticity of SALARY with respect to POINTS rises from .205 to .321 in the period of free agency compared to the period of quasi-monopsony, an increase of more than 50 percent. An F-test reveals that the difference is significant at the .071 percent level ($F = 3.26$). This result is adequate but not as strong as in baseball. The reasons for the weaker result lie in the weaker statistical significance of the covariates and in the creeping competitiveness in the players' market during the mid-1970s. Some of the effect can be discerned from the slope dummy for the years 1973–75 times POINTS (a similar slope dummy on SUMMINS proved statistically insignificant). The value of that slope dummy is $9.436E-02$. Adding the two slopes together shows that the elasticity of SALARY with respect to POINTS in the 1973–75 period is .299, which is not much smaller than in the period of free agency. It is apparent that increased player mobility expanded the hierarchical wage structure in basketball. For example, in 1970 Kareem Abdul-Jabbar made (in 1991 dollars) $871,066 compared to $64,200 for the lowest-paid player. The ratio of highest to lowest salary was 13.6. In 1975 Bill Walton at Portland and Moses Malone at Utah made $1.508 million, which gives a ratio to the lowest-paid player of 23.5. In the period of free agency, Magic Johnson in the 1988–89 season with the Lakers made $3.6 million (in 1991 dollars) compared to $88,100 for the lowest-paid player in the sample (ratio equals 40.8).

The coefficient of SALARY with respect to SUMMINS rises by about a third, from $3.811E-05$ in the period 1968–1975 to $5.106E-05$ in the period 1984–88. An F-test reveals that the difference is significant ($F = 4.27$) at the .039 percent level. The SUMMINS**2 coefficient changes substantially from $-6.592E-10$ to $-3.405E-10$. An F-test on the difference yielded $F = 6.97$, which is significant at the .008 percent level. A joint F-test on the constant term, POINTS, SUMMINS, and SUMMINS**2 was also statistically significant ($F = 288.1$). The other performance measures do not bear up as well. REBOUNDS is not significant in the earnings function for the period 1968–75; ASSISTS has a negative sign in the period 1984–1988.

Wage and Performance Profiles

There are several salient features about the career profiles of sportsmen. Except in rare instances most players entering the major leagues are untested rookies whose path of performance is uncertain.

Baseball players spend several years in the minor leagues developing their talent. Pay is low during this period of training; player investment in developing talent is considerable. Players with good records in the minor leagues tend to be promoted to the major leagues. Performance in the minor leagues is not a perfect screen for prospective performance in the major leagues; players often appear on major league rosters for a short period and then return to the minor leagues for further seasoning. When a player secures a permanent place on a major league roster, he tends to play infrequently for a few years, and often he is traded to another club. After a time, if the player is judged superior, he plays more frequently. Player performance tends to rise over a certain portion of the playing career, reach a peak, and then decline. The rise in performance in the early portion of a career may be partly due to learning by doing, but more likely it is due to player and club investments in honing playing skills (realized talent). The decline in performance is due to the deterioration of reflexes, sight, speed, and so on that aging brings. The age at which the decline in playing skills sets in, and perhaps its rate, ought to be affected by player investments in skill and conditioning later in the career life cycle.

In basketball (and football) the minor leagues are the college circuit. Realized talent (again the player investment can be substantial—players are paid tuition, room, and board while playing in the college circuit) in college play determines one's standing in the college-player draft. A player who makes an NBA club spends several years playing irregularly. As in baseball, realized talent (performance) is expected to rise during the early years of regular play in the NBA, reach a maximum, and then decline. The reasons for the life-cycle pattern in productivity are similar to those in baseball, although the weights on the attributes of performance may differ (e.g., speed and endurance may be more valuable in basketball than in baseball).

Thus the life-cycle pattern of earnings is the outcome of a team rank-order tournament. Players of high talent endogenously invest in the development of their skills and determine their chance of securing positions as regular players, who earn considerably more than irregular players. An empirical issue is whether pay is less than productivity in the early portion of the career and greater than productivity in the later portion, and if so, whether the liberalization

Table 2.3 GLS Estimates of Life-Cycle Earnings and Performance in Baseball

Variables	1964–75 ln TOTBASES	1977–92 ln TOTBASES	1964–75 ln SALARY	1977–92 ln SALARY
CONSTANT	3.655	4.122	3.694	11.557
	(44.28)	(72.01)	(138.27)	(386.32)
SUMGAMES	2.273E–03	2.378E–03	1.443E–03	3.820E–03
	(12.54)	(17.95)	(19.99)	(40.81)
SUMGAMES**2	−7.120E–07	−8.820E–07	−3.100E–07	−1.246E–06
	(8.66)	(13.83)	(8.24)	(22.08)
YEAR DUMMIES	No	No	Yes	Yes
R^2	.274	.258	.637	.708
N	873	1,895	873	1,895

of the rules for allocating playing talent have changed the parameters of the team rank-order tournament model in a meaningful fashion.

A second issue (confirmed in the parameter estimates in tables 2.1 and 2.2) is that one does observe that aging players tend to experience a reduction in pay relative to a prior peak. As realized playing talent declines with age, players are either retired or stay on for a while at a lower salary. For example, when Pat Cummings was 28 years old, the Dallas Mavericks paid him $800,000 (1984–85 season). At age 32 the Knicks paid him $525,000 (1988–89 season). Dave Winfield made $3.75 million in his last year with the California Angels (1991). Toronto paid him $2.3 million in 1992 mainly to serve as a designated hitter. Earnie Whitt's salary fell from $1.2 million in Atlanta in 1990 to $300,000 in Baltimore in 1991. There may be a selectivity bias here; some aging players whose performance is in decline may choose to retire rather than face a substantial pay cut to stay on for another season or two.

To clarify these issues, life-cycle earnings and performance profiles were estimated for the monopsony and competitive periods. Because the change in the player allocation rules is sharp in baseball but fuzzy in basketball, the analysis is confined to baseball. These estimated profiles are presented in table 2.3. SUMGAMES and SUMGAMES**2 are the main regressors. The independent variables are linear; the dependent variables are logarithmic. Estimation is by generalized least squares.

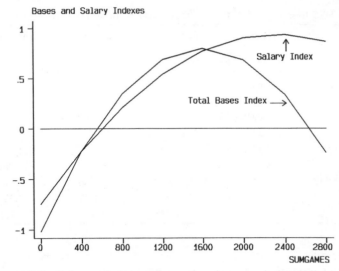

Figure 2.3   Indexes of player salary and performance in baseball, 1964–75.

The slope of TOTBASES with respect to SUMGAMES is steeper under free agency ($2.38E-03$ versus $2.27E-03$) and much steeper for SALARY with respect to SUMGAMES ($3.82E-03$ versus $1.44E-03$). The peak in performance is 1,596 career games (about 10.6 years of play at 150 games per year) in the period 1964–75 compared to 1,347 career games (about 9 years of play) for the 1977–92 period. The peak in salary is at 2,328 career games (15.5 years of play) in the monopsony period, and at 1,523 games (10.2 years of play) in the period of free agency. The difference in the coefficients (a joint test on SUMGAMES and SUMGAMES**2) is highly significant (an F-value in the performance equations of 21.08 and in the salary equations of 575.69). The sharp increase in the hierarchy of earnings in baseball under free agency has induced greater player investment in developing playing skills more rapidly; players thus tend to realize their maximum potential performance about a year and a half earlier than during the monopsony period.

The wage and performance profiles in the two periods are shown in figures 2.3 and 2.4. These profiles are indexed to the respective geometric means. The performance profile is a productivity index

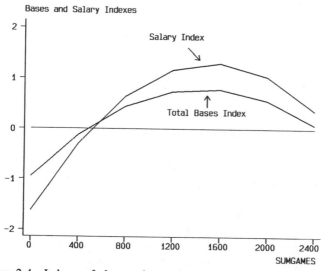

Figure 2.4 Indexes of player salary and performance in baseball, 1977–92.

for the representative player over the playing career. Because the index is normalized (divided by the mean), it may be viewed as an index of player marginal revenue product.[13] In the 1964–75 period, the index of player pay exceeds the index of player marginal revenue product until 405 career games (about 2.7 years for regular players). From that number of career games up to 1,550 career games (about 10.3 years in the majors), productivity exceeds pay, which is an indication of monopsonistic exploitation. Somewhat beyond the peak of performance for the representative player, earnings exceed productivity.

The earnings/productivity profiles under free agency contrast sharply. The index of player marginal revenue product exceeds that of earnings up to 547 career games (about 3.6 years). Thereafter earnings exceed productivity, as in the bonding model. Note that the gap between pay and performance after the crossover point is much more substantial during the period of free agency than in the monopsony period. Also observe the closer proximity of the peaks in performance and salary under free agency than in the monopsony period.

Conclusions

The team rank-order tournament is an ideal framework for analyzing the sports labor market. This is so because productivity is easily measured in sports (unless there are important complementarities of inputs, as in football), and the relationship between individual performance and club output (the win percent) or revenue is transparent. Also, the need to create incentives for players to optimize investment in playing skills and maximize effort per contest is recognized as important to club profit. While the sequencing of one-on-one contests is not directly observable in baseball or basketball, as it is in golf or tennis, the variables TOTBASES and POINTS and SUMGAMES and SUMMINS capture the essence of a rank-order tournament of serially repeated contests for starting and backup positions. Club owners, managers, and coaches choose player personnel for starting positions on the basis of expected performance. High performance has greater value to a club because it correlates with winning. Superior performance arises not only from raw athletic talent but from investments in playing skills and in effort per contest. The intrateam salary structure determines the optimal investment in playing skills. As starters, highly skilled players play more games in baseball and more minutes per game in basketball than backup players.

A hierarchical wage structure has always existed in professional team sports. During the monopsony period in sports, the ratio of the highest- to lowest-paid player was on the order of 10; now it is on the order of 50. The greater payoff for investment in playing skills appears to have induced greater investments by players. In baseball the peak in performance appears to occur about a year and a half earlier in the modern period. Because clubs must now compete for free agents, that competition has led to a much earlier peak in player salary (about five years earlier) that corresponds closely to the peak in player performance.

▼ The Distribution of Player Earnings

▼

Introduction

The distribution of earnings in the economy has been linked to a variety of exogenous and endogenous factors: innate ability, motivation, acquired human capital, skill, occupation, race, sex, unionization, mobility, work/leisure preference, risk preference, luck, and so on. In sports the governance structure, or rule space, will be shown to have a large effect on the distribution of player earnings within and across sports. The distribution of player earnings is affected by the distribution of athletic talent, the playing rules of the sport (to the extent that they affect the set of athletic attributes and the substitutability of those attributes), the nature of the production function in the sport, the labor market rules for allocating player talent, and the revenue-sharing rule in the league.

In the economy, individuals are endowed with talent or acquire skill through investment and training that is to be utilized in productive activities. The realization of an individual's talent in an activity is his or her performance. The dimensions of talent are too numerous and perhaps too mysterious to be precisely quantified, but it is convenient to think of talent as being composed of broad dimensions like intelligence, strength and coordination, and further refinements of these dimensions (e.g., language, math, or reasoning ability). In this way an individual's "talent" for a particular activity can be thought of as a weighted total of the dimensional attributes he or she possesses, where the weight of each dimension is determined by the market for the activity.

In production activities, the weights (rewards per unit) placed on the dimensions of talent are determined by derived demand, through production technology, by the supplies of the attributes of talent, and by the organization of the talent market (rules that compensate the various dimensions of talent). Where the rules of the talent market are the same for all, the distribution of income is a function of the distribution of performance that is weighted by effort. This is most transparent in piecework activities, where performance can be measured as output per period, and effort can be measured as the number of periods committed to piecework activities. Then if one controls for effort, income is a scalar multiple (determined by the value of output) of performance, and the distribution of income and the distribution of performance are identical.

Within different talent markets, unique characteristics make for predictable changes in the relation between the distribution of talent and income. For example, when the payments for performance are rank-ordered (that is, where the margin of performance between individuals determines their rank in the payment hierarchy but not the margin of compensation), income will be only rank-correlated with performance, and the distribution of income will (depending on the payment schedule) correspond more or less to the distribution of performance. In team production settings, where the assessment of individual performance is more difficult, or where the consequence of the employment of effort and talent is uncertain, the distribution of income tends to be more equal than in piecework settings. Finally, when there are rents (defined as returns not associated with the application of productive talent) to be distributed, income and its distribution may bear little resemblance to the underlying distribution of performance.

Here we examine the effects of the rules of the game on the distribution of player earnings in the sports economy. The focus is on the effect of the rule space on the earnings of athletes, which is attractive for several reasons. First, the rules of the game in sports are known, and in some sports they have undergone substantial change. Second, the dimensions of athletic performance and the technology of production, although complex, lends itself to fairly unambiguous modeling. Finally, data exist to test some propositions about the effects of some rules on the distribution of earnings within and across sports. The main factor that has changed in sports over the period in which player salary data exist is the compensation formula for salaries (player reservation versus free agency). Several other factors affect the distribution of player pay, however, and these will also be considered. Implicit in the discussion of player salary distribution here is the model developed in the previous chapter.

The Distribution of Talent

Like most human characteristics, athletic ability is normally distributed. It is likely that this ability is multidimensional. Conceptually we may think of some multidimensional metric of athletic talent, T, as a function of a vector of independent athletic abilities, t_i: $T = T(t_i)$. The set of attributes includes speed, agility, reflexes, aggressiveness, cunning, strength, coordination, stamina, perception, intelligence, size, and other attributes that in combination make up athletic ability. The distribution of these attributes also is normal. Depending on the technology of the sport, these athletic attributes may be independent, complements, or substitutes. The distribution (variance) of athletic ability is simply the sum of the variances of the attributes of athletic ability and the covariance between them. If athletic attributes are independent, random variables, then the covariance is zero. If athletic attributes are substitutes (complements), then the covariance term is negative (positive). Conventional wisdom among sports kinesiologists is that many athletic attributes are substitutes. However the rarity (less rare today) of players in one sport playing in or switching to another suggests that not all athletic attributes are substitutes (e.g., there are few seven-foot baseball players or 325-pound basketball players). Investments in developing playing talent and learning by doing in a sport play a role in enhancing specific athletic attributes. There may be an element of athletic asset-specificity in a particular sport.

While it is true that professional athletes have levels of most athletic attributes that are in the upper tail, it is not necessarily true that each athlete has more or less the same level of each attribute. Some athletes may be extraordinarily gifted in one or a few of the attributes, say speed and agility, but be only average among professional athletes in some of the other attributes. For example, Spud Webb, who played for the Atlanta Hawks, at 5'7" and 135 pounds, was much too short and light for the NBA, yet through extraordinary agility and jumping power, he was able to score against bigger opponents.

Generally the greater the number of attributes that constitute athletic performance and the greater the degree of substitutability (or, the lesser the degree of positive correlation) among those attributes, the more equal is the distribution of athletic talent in a sport. To the extent that earnings are correlated with athletic talent, the flatter the distribution of athletic talent in a sport, the more equal is the distribution of earnings within a sport.

The Nature of the Production Function in the Sport

Player skills interact with one another in team sports. The degree of interaction among player skills determines the nature of the production function. If player input is unambiguously measured and largely independent of other player inputs (an additively separable production function), the player's contribution to team wins or revenue is known. In baseball the contest is mainly between pitcher and batter. Because of the great number of contests, there is large variance in pitching and hitting performance: a pitcher (hitter) faces the same hitter (pitcher) a minuscule number of times. Individual performance can be accurately measured.

If the production technology is not additive, but exhibits complementarity among inputs, then the individual contribution to team output (revenue) cannot be measured accurately. Two implications for player salary arise in sports with a high degree of player interaction (team production). First, because individual performance is subject to measurement error (noise), the additional variance in the measurement of performance tends to decrease the inequality in the distribution of earnings, depending on the difference in talent between players.[1] Second, the returns from the interactive effects of team play are captured by management through the coaching function, not by the players. Other things being equal, this implies that player share of revenue is negatively correlated with the degree of player interaction in team sports.

In football the interaction of players is crucial to team performance. Not only does the complementarity of input in football make it difficult to truly allocate, say, rushing yards gained between the running back and the offensive line and downfield blockers, the team aspects of production tend to lessen the contribution of the outstanding players and improve the performance of the less outstanding players. For example, a premier offensive player will draw the attention of all of the defense and permit lesser players to excel. A premier defensive player may occupy two blockers and leave another player unattended.

Basketball and hockey tend to fall between baseball and football in the degree of complementarity of player inputs. As in baseball, basketball and hockey players compete with the same players on numerous occasions. Points (goals) scored, field-goal and free-throw percentage, assists, blocked shots, and rebounds give an indication of the individuals' contributions. In both sports, however, interaction among teammates who are all (except the goalie) active and potential scorers at each point in the contest is more important than in baseball.

The greater the degree of complementarity of inputs into team production, the more the team is subject to exploitation of its weakest link by opponents. Exploitation of the weak link is seen most often in football, but it also occurs in basketball and hockey. Perhaps the best example of weak-link technology is auto racing. The success of a racing team is determined by the performance of its weakest input. The best driver cannot compensate for a poor mechanic or pit crew, and a superior mechanic or pit crew cannot make up for poor driving. In auto, boat, or horse racing there is a tendency for inputs to sort themselves into teams with homogeneous talent among inputs, because acquiring a more talented input at any position has value only if that position is the weak link on the team.

Complementarity of inputs and weak-link technology, by reducing the contribution of specific individual talent to team output or reducing the marginal contribution of inputs to that of the weakest link, tends to make the distribution of earnings more equal. Thus on the basis of the description of team production in the team sports, one would expect the distribution of earnings to be more equal among football players than among baseball players. In the weak-link-technology sports like auto racing, one would expect the distribution of earnings to be more equal than in sports not subject to weak-link production, as in singles tennis or golf. Sorting and matching among teams in automobile, horse, and boat racing will ameliorate the effect of weak-link technology.

The Influence of the Playing Rules of the Sport

The vector of athletic attributes for a club relative to the league athletic talent yields the club's win percentage. As I have argued, these attributes are mainly substitutes. Playing rules act as parameters that enhance or constrain different attributes of play. In the early history of sports, play was aggressive and rough, and injury was commonplace. One feature of playing rules is that they constrain player aggressiveness (infractions) by assigning penalties (a Pigouvian tax) for rough play. Referees (independent judges) are hired to enforce the rules and assign the prescribed penalties. By raising the probability of club victory or attracting fans, aggressive play has value, and human nature being what it is, players push at the margin of rough play. In some sports, such as hockey, rough and aggressive play is rewarded.[2] Sometimes the aggressive play becomes more subtle and makes refereeing more difficult. This has led to increased importance for the role of refereeing in sports and a class of professional referees.

Some fouling in sports has high value but is associated with injury. In football the kicker at the moment of the punt, the quarterback at the moment of the pass, the receiver at the moment of the catch, and the runner at the moment of being downed are particularly vulnerable to injury. In hockey, checking against the boards and the hockey stick induce injury. Penalties are assigned against the offending player (team) as compensation to the injured player (team). By lowering the net value of aggressive play, penalties reduce the value of that dimension of athletic ability.

Changes in playing rules may broaden or narrow the range of attributes that contribute to performance. The twenty-four-second clock rule in basketball speeded up play and increased the value of ball handling, passing, and tighter team play, while the three-point rule introduced long-range accuracy as a valuable input. In football the forward pass increased the value of the quarterback and made speed of the receiver a valuable input. In baseball, pitcher dominance is attenuated by rule changes concerning the strike zone, distance and height of the pitching mound, the banning of certain types of pitches, a penalty for pitching high and inside on the batter, and so on.

The effects of playing rules and changes in these rules on the distribution of earnings within a sport depend on their effects on the distribution of talent. To the extent that a playing rule decreases the substitutability of playing attributes, the effect of the rule is to make the distribution of athletic talent more skewed. This increased dispersion in athletic ability increases the dispersion of earnings. To the extent that a playing rule increases the set of playing attributes or increases the substitutability of attributes, the effect is to increase the equality of the earnings distribution.

Randomness of outcome is a feature of all sports. The greater the degree of chance in the outcome, the lower the correlation between athletic talent and club standing, because it is less likely that superior talent will yield the desired performance outcome. Randomness of outcome weakens the correlation between performance and pay. The theoretical standard deviation of the mean win percent is inversely proportional to the square root of the number of games. In baseball, with a 162-game season, the randomness of outcome is low (about a third of that for football), while in football, with a 16-game schedule, randomness is highest. Basketball and hockey, with half the games of baseball, have more randomness of outcome than baseball but less than football. Moreover, the play-off format in football—that of sudden death—yields more randomness of outcome than the seven-game format in baseball and basketball. Thus sports with fewer contests should have more income equality and less of a correlation between the distribution of talent and the distribution of earnings. Baseball, basketball, and hockey will tend to have a more skewed distribution than football because of the lower variance of random outcome due to the longer season and the play-off format.

Contests in individual sports have two basic formats: match play and play against the field of competitors. In match play there are seedings, as in tennis tournaments, which pit the best players against weaker opponents in the early rounds.

Consider a large competitive field, where the distribution of performances is nearly continuous and has little variance, even though individual performance may have a large variance. Assume that seeding accurately reflects the ranking of individual average performance. Against a field of competitors, the individual's performance variability determines the variability of his or her finish among the field (higher than ranked when performance is better than average and lower than ranked when performance is poorer than average), because across the entire field of competitors the distribution of performance is fairly constant. For example, the distribution of scores in golf matches is fairly constant, even though individual players' finishes vary widely across matches.

In seeded play each ranked player faces lower-ranked opponents until the round of the contest that eliminates the fraction of contests that contains the fractile of the contestant's ranking. Except for upsets, the player then faces higher-ranked players. In seeded play the variance of finish about one's rank is less than in play-against-the-field contests.

Leband shows that the probability of a top-ranked player finishing in first place is about four times higher in tennis than in golf.[3] Suppose that there are one hundred players in tournaments and that the talent distribution is identical in both sports. The top competitors are in the upper 5 percent of the tail of the distribution (two standard deviations from the mean), and let them be equally good. In golf the top five beat all others, and one of them is the winner. The probability that one of the five top-ranked players will win the tournament is .2. The probability of one of the top five winning the tournament in a seven-round match-play tennis tournament is $.96^7 = .75$.

Because the probability that the top player(s) will win (place) the tournament is much higher in seeded play than in play against the field, seeded match play tends to increase the inequality of the distribution of income relative to play against the field whenever the prize schedule is convex with respect to player finish. All else being equal, the distribution of earnings in tennis should be more skewed than in golf.

The Influence of the Division of Revenue in Team Sports

Clubs earn revenue (gate receipts and broadcast income) from at home (H) and away (A) games. The amount of revenue earned is highly correlated with the club's win percent, $R = R(W)$. If α is the share of revenue from home games and $1 - \alpha$ is the share from away games, club revenue is

$$R(W) = \alpha R_H(W) + (1 - \alpha)R_A(W).$$

The increment in revenue associated with an increment in the win percent is

$$MR(W) = \alpha MR_H(W) - (1 - \alpha)MR_A(W).[4]$$

The division of revenues is the most extreme in hockey and is the most even in football. Baseball and basketball have an uneven division of revenue, but it is less uneven than in hockey.

Consider the effect of revenue division on a club's financial incentive to win and hence the players' contribution to incremental club revenue through their performance. In hockey and substantially in baseball and basketball, all or nearly all of the incremental revenue from an increase in the win record accrues to the team. In football, where the home and away split approaches 50–50, the incremental revenue from an increment in wins approaches zero. With a 50–50 division of revenues among clubs, there is no correlation between the distribution of talent and the distribution of club revenue. With a 100–0 division of revenue, the correlation between the distribution of talent and revenue is very high.

Whatever the rule for allocating player talent within a league (player reservation as in hockey, Plan-B free agency in football until 1992, or free agency for veterans in baseball and basketball), the more equal the revenue division among the clubs, the less is the correspondence between a player's contribution to incremental club revenue and his pay. If players are free to move between clubs and the division of revenues is 100–0, a player's pay tends to rise to the expected incremental revenue to the club from that player's performance. If players are free to move and the division of revenue is 50–50, there is no relationship between player salary and player incremental revenue. If players are bound to their clubs (reserved) and the division of revenues is 100–0, player salaries are not equal, but are functionally related to player contribution to club incremental revenue. Player reservation in a league with an even division of revenues may result in lower average pay for the players but adds nothing further to the effect on the distribution of earnings among the players.

In general the smaller the share of revenue going to the home club, the lower the incremental value of winning, and hence the lower the incremental value of superior player performance. The effect of socialization of revenues is to reduce the inequality of earnings among players.

The Influence of the Sport's Labor-Market Rules

In the absence of league restrictions on player-initiated movement, a minimum rookie wage, and a share of revenue for the visiting competitor, interclub competition for playing talent will tend to bid player salaries toward the level of the players' expected contribution to incremental club revenue. Restrictions on player-initiated movement convey monopsony power to the team owning the exclusive right to the player's service. Player reservation results in player salary less than player marginal revenue product, with the club owner pocketing the monopsony rent. Under monopsony, player earnings are still correlated with player talent, but the evidence indicates that restrictions on player-initiated mobility depress the pay of the star players more than the pay of journeymen players.[5] Hence the earnings distribution among players subject to restrictions on mobility is expected to be flatter than among players who are free to move where they choose.

In team sports incremental club revenue is associated with the fans' desire for wins. With or without restrictions on player mobility or revenue sharing among the clubs, players need to be motivated to perform at their highest level. A hierarchical wage structure with a wide differential between starters and backup players as described in the previous chapter induces players to perform at their best. This hierarchy of pay is correlated with the talent distribution. Thus, even in a sport with completely socialized revenue and a reserve clause, pay and performance will be correlated. Under a system of player reservation, however, the club owner obtains most of the rents associated with superstar performance; under free agency, the player obtains most of the rents associated with his performance.

All team sports have minimum rookie salaries, and basketball has a team salary cap. Rookie players may not play at all, or they may play infrequently. Such players have value both in their potential and in their availability to substitute for regular players because of injury, foul trouble, and so on. In some instances a minimum salary for rookies may yield pay above marginal revenue product. If so, the effect of the minimum wage is to make the earnings distribution somewhat flatter than the talent (marginal revenue) distribution.

In theory an effective salary cap truncates the financial ability of a team to purchase superior player talent. The roster cost of journeymen players will never exceed the salary cap; it is when a free-agent superstar is recruited that a salary cap may impede a team's ability to land that player. If there are a sufficient number of basketball superstars in the market and teams competing for their services, the salary cap may depress the salary offers to these players. If so, a team salary cap acts as a tax on superstar salaries, and hence reduces earnings inequality among players.

In tournament sports the structure of competition (seeded versus play against the field) and the prize schedule affect the distribution of player income. The more equally distributed the prizes in a sport, the more equal the distribution of earnings among competitors, other things being equal. In horse racing nearly two-thirds of the prize money usually goes to the winner, and prizes are only awarded for the first four finishes. Other competitors in the race receive nothing. In golf 18 percent of the prize money usually goes to the winner (a little more than a third of the purse to the top three finishers). In tennis about half of the purse money goes to the top four finishers. In auto racing the first-place share is comparatively small, and the purse is more evenly split over the field.

To be attractive a tournament must have a minimum field of competitors. Where opportunity costs of the participants are high, the prize distribution must be sufficiently flat to induce entry by the least likely winners. In golf and tennis, opportunity costs are relatively low—lost wages and low transportation, lodging, and equipment costs. Amateurs often compete in these contests and expect no prize money. In automobile racing opportunity costs are very high. Typically it costs about $10 million to field "Indy" cars over the seventeen-race CART season. On average, it costs about $3 million to field cars for the twenty-four-race NASCAR circuit. To attract a field of competitors, auto racing must offer greater prizes to those at the bottom end of the field at the expense of the top finishers. Relative to golf and tennis, the distribution of income in automobile racing is expected to be flatter.

Finally, the earnings distribution in individual sports is expected to be more skewed than in team sports. First, because no prize money awaits the bottom finishers in individual sports, but at least a minimum salary is available to rookies in team sports, earnings inequality is higher in individual sports. Second, the top earners in individual sports sometimes earn more than the top earners in team sports. Race driver Ayrton Senna earned a base salary of $15 million from McLaren International. Sugar Ray Leonard earned $27.5 million in prize money, and Mike Tyson earned $22.1 million. Moreover there are differences in the degree of risks borne by superstars in team and in individual sports. Potentially, there is large variance in athletic performance over time. When the team accepts the risk, as with guaranteed long-term contracts, some of the risk premium is collected by the club in the form of reduced superstar player salary. When the player accepts the risk, as in the individual sports, the risk premium is collected by the player. Of course appearance guarantees help mitigate risk.

Predictions

The preceding analysis yields several predictions about the distribution of earnings in sports that are useful to summarize. First, for team sports the greatest inequality in the distribution of earnings should occur in baseball. It has extensive veteran free agency, separable player performance, modest revenue sharing, and hence extensive opportunities for increasing team-specific revenues through team performance. Somewhat lesser inequality is expected in basketball, which differs from baseball in several significant ways: it has a higher minimum salary requirement, the team salary cap may lower the maximum income earned by the superstars, and the somewhat greater team production in basketball implies that player performance is not entirely separable. On the other hand, the possibility of dominance by a single player is greater because of the small size of basketball teams. The distribution of income among players in football will be more equal than in baseball and basketball because of limited free agency until 1993, highly interactive player performance effects, and extensive revenue sharing. In hockey the distribution of earnings should be more equal than in any other league sport. It has the most restrictive player reserve clause, no viable alternative leagues, interactive player-performance effects, and it generates significantly less revenue.

Second, among the individual sports with seeded match play, tennis earnings will be less equally distributed than in golf, where play is against the field of competitors. Between men's and women's tennis, the distribution of earnings should be somewhat less equal among the men because the greater reliance on five-set matches reduces measurement error. Because tournament prizes are roughly equivalent and the nature of play does not differ, the relative distributions of income in men's and women's golf should be roughly similar. The distribution of winnings will be most equal in auto racing. While the earnings data are for the drivers, it is a team sport characterized by weak-link performance technology, and despite the ameliorating effects of sorting and matching team members, imperfect matching will tend to reduce distributional inequality. Additionally, auto racing has a high opportunity cost of participation that, for given value, forces race sponsors to offer a more equal distribution of the rank-order prizes. Finally, inequality in the distribution of earnings will be greater in the individual sports than in the team sports.

The Distribution of Earnings in the Sports

First examined is the distribution of earnings in professional team sports.[6] In table 3.1 the distribution of recent player salaries in baseball, basketball, football, and hockey is given in quintiles, and the Gini coefficient, a summary inequality measure of the distribution, is presented. The Lorenz curves for these sports are presented in figure 3.1. Examination of the table and the figure reveal that the distribution of earnings is more equal in hockey and football than in basketball and baseball. Specific statistical testing of differences in the Lorenz curves reveals a transitive ranking of earnings inequality, with baseball highest, followed by basketball, football, and hockey.[7]

The effect of free agency on the earnings distributions in baseball

Table 3.1   Earnings and Talent Distributions in Sports

Sport	Q1	Q2	Q3	Q4	Q5	Gini Coefficient
Earnings						
Baseball, 1990	3.4	4.9	12.2	26.2	53.4	.5097
Baseball, 1973	6.4	10.5	15.3	23.5	44.2	.3715
Basketball, 1989–90	4.6	9.7	14.6	23.1	48.0	.4233
Basketball, 1967–68	9.0	12.6	18.3	22.0	38.1	.2739
Football, 1990	6.1	10.7	15.1	21.3	46.8	.3994
Football, 1992	6.2	11.6	16.0	22.6	43.6	.3678
Hockey, 1990	10.2	13.4	16.8	21.8	37.8	.2748
Hockey, 1978	11.4	14.6	17.8	21.9	34.3	.2237
PGA, 1990	0.3	2.4	10.2	23.1	64.1	.6329
LPGA, 1990	0.7	3.5	9.7	20.5	65.7	.6392
ATP, 1990	5.4	8.1	12.9	21.1	52.5	.4671
WTA, 1990	5.1	6.9	9.3	15.2	63.6	.5550
Auto racing, 1990	5.1	9.8	14.6	22.0	48.6	.4105
Talent						
Baseball, 1989	1.0	6.1	15.8	29.3	47.9	.4775
Baseball, 1972	0.9	5.7	15.4	29.8	49.0	.5008
Basketball, 1988	0.8	5.5	13.8	27.7	52.2	.5202
Basketball, 1967	2.1	9.3	17.1	27.5	44.0	.4140

and in basketball is shown in table 3.1 and in figure 3.2. The Lorenz curves for the salary distributions in baseball are for 1973 and 1990, and those for basketball are for 1967–68 and 1989–90. The year 1973 was selected for baseball because it is the year prior to the introduction of salary arbitration.[8] The 1967–68 season was selected for NBA basketball because it was the first year of competition with the ABA, and the labor-market rule was as restrictive as in baseball.[9] Clearly, free agency has made the salary distributions more unequal in both sports (the differences in the Lorenz curves are statistically significant). The Gini coefficient in baseball rose from .37 to .51.[10] In basketball, earnings inequality rose from .27 to .42. Thus we can conclude that the switch from a restricted to a freer labor market in baseball and basketball increased the inequality of earnings among

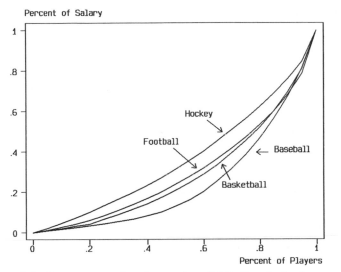

Figure 3.1   Lorenz curves for player salary distributions in the four professional team sports, 1990.

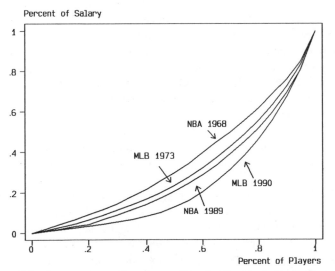

Figure 3.2   Lorenz curves for player salary distribution in baseball and basketball, before and after free agency.

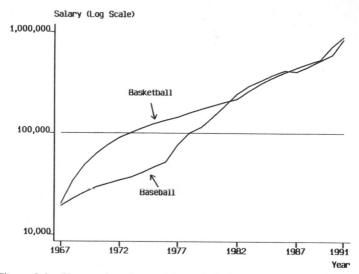

Figure 3.3   Player salary (log scale) trends in baseball and basketball, 1967–91.

the players. The salary distributions of hockey players in the 1978 and 1990 seasons were also compared. While the difference in the Lorenz curves is statistically significant, the magnitude of change is small (note the change in the Gini from .22 to .27). For football no long-term comparisons are possible. Quirk and Fort calculated the Gini coefficient for the NFL for 1988 at .411.[11] For 1990 (1992) the coefficient in table 3.1 is .40 (.37). Plan-B free agency increased the relative earnings of the nonprotected players. With the 1993 owner-player collective bargaining agreement, increased freedom of movement for players will tend to increase inequality of salary in the NFL. Free-agent salaries will rise dramatically, and rookie salaries will be restrained, thereby substantially raising the inequality of player earnings.

Veteran free agency has led to a dramatic increase in player salaries and has made the salary distributions more unequal in baseball and basketball. The trend in baseball and basketball salaries is shown in figure 3.3, which is in log scale for better resolution. Player salaries grew at a higher rate in basketball due to interleague competition. In 1967 mean salaries were close in both sports ($19,000

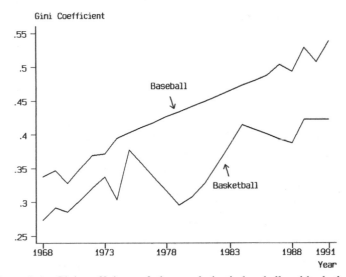

Figure 3.4   Gini coefficients of player salaries in baseball and basketball, 1968–91.

in baseball, $20,000 in basketball). Hockey players made about $19,100, and football players about $25,000 in 1967. By 1972 basketball players were making $90,000, and baseball players $34,100. Hockey players made about $37,000, and football players about $35,000 in 1972. Baseball salaries took off in 1976 with veteran free agency, while basketball salaries rose rapidly after free agency in 1982. It was in this period that hockey and football salaries began to lag behind those of baseball and basketball. By the mid-1980s salary parity existed in the two sports. The Gini coefficient in baseball was more than a third larger in 1990 compared to 1973. In basketball the Gini coefficient was more than a half larger in 1989 compared to 1967. The trend in the Gini coefficient in both sports is shown in figure 3.4. Thus the switch from a restricted to a freer labor market in baseball and basketball accelerated player salary growth and increased the inequality of earnings among the players.

It has been argued that the distribution of pay and performance should be more proximate in a freer labor market than in a restricted labor market, but to demonstrate this requires a measure of performance. There is no single metric in baseball or in basketball. As a

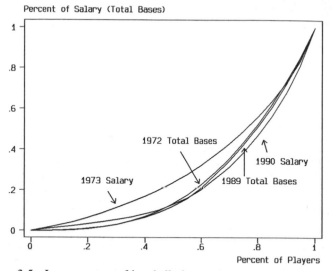

Percent of Salary (Total Bases)

Figure 3.5   Lorenz curves of baseball player salary and total bases distributions, before and after free agency.

crude measure for baseball, total bases advanced during the season for each hitter were calculated.[12] For basketball the measure is total points scored. The robustness of the performance measure is not an issue of great importance. Certainly the measures are reasonable metrics of player performance, and are probably correlated with other dimensions of player ability. More important, the point of the exercise is to compare the distributions of the performance measures and the distributions of earnings in the setting of a restricted and then a relatively free labor market.

Table 3.1 and figure 3.5 show the Lorenz curves of the salary and total base distributions for 1973 and 1990. Salary for the 1973 season is significantly more equally distributed than total bases in the 1972 season, when the reserve clause was in effect. In the 1990 season, which was characterized by a freer labor market, the salary and total base Lorenz curves are not statistically different from each other.

For basketball, the Lorenz curves of salary and total points scored appear in table 3.1 and figure 3.6. For the period prior to free agency (1967–68), salary is more equally distributed than total points (Ginis

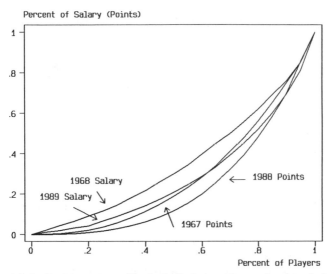

Figure 3.6 Lorenz curves of basketball player salary and points, before and after free agency.

of .27 versus .41). For the era of free agency, salary still is more equally distributed than total points scored, but the gap has narrowed (Ginis of .42 versus .52). While the inequality of earnings has risen in basketball, so has the inequality of total points scored. The rise in the inequality of points scored may be related to the large expansion in the number of NBA clubs (more than a doubling). Talent was spread more thinly in the later than in the earlier period, as clubs had to dig deeper into the athletic ability distribution. This may also be due to the effect of team salary caps on the salaries of superstar players. The superstars contribute relatively more to team output and receive relatively less in salary.

The distributions of earnings in some of the individual sports are given in table 3.1.[13] Some caution must be exercised in interpreting the results for the individual sports in the table. The earnings samples in men's and women's tennis are truncated (the top 150 finishers). The population is unknown. Since the earnings of the lower-income participants are under-represented, comparisons in tennis are problematic. The earnings in golf are a complete rendition.

There is no clear transitive ranking between men's and women's

Table 3.2 Earnings Distribution in Individual Sports for the Top 150 Prize Winners

Sport	Quintiles					Gini Coefficient
	Q1	Q2	Q3	Q4	Q5	
Earnings						
PGA, 1990	7.2	10.5	14.4	21.5	46.5	.3734
LPGA, 1990	2.9	6.3	11.8	20.3	58.7	.5419
ATP, 1990	7.5	10.0	14.3	20.0	48.2	.3961
WTA, 1990	5.1	9.8	14.6	22.0	48.6	.5550

golf. The tails of the Lorenz distributions cross (note that the Gini coefficients are nearly identical). The distribution of prize money is similar, and the rules are the same, so it is not surprising that the distributions are similar. Using golf for comparison, the Lorenz dominance tests reveal that there is greater earnings inequality in individual sports than in the team sports. This is probably the result of the ability to vary labor effort in individual sports. The distribution of driver winnings in auto racing Lorenz-dominates that of golf presumably because of the high opportunity cost of auto racing.

Table 3.2 compares the earnings distributions of the top 150 prize winners in golf and tennis. Rank-ordering of these distributions is not possible because of a significant crossing after the first ordinate. However, except for the first ordinate in the distribution of men's tennis, golf dominates tennis in all of the other ordinates. Obviously, since the earnings in the lower quintile are not fully observed, comparisons with the first quintile are spurious. The results offer weak evidence for the proposition that play against the field yields greater equality in the distribution than seeded match play.

△

△

△ PART THREE

▼ The Market for Sports Franchises

▼

▼

△ **F O U R**

▼   Of Winners and Losers:

Momentum in Sports
▼

Introduction

Empirical evidence of the historical distribution of the win percent among clubs shows a lack of competitive balance. Using the standard deviation of the win percent as a measure of competitive balance, I showed the lack of balance in major league baseball in a previous study.[1] Quirk and Fort have utilized this measure also, and show a lack of competitive balance in other league sports.[2]

The attractiveness of the measure arises partly from the fact that it can be compared to the theoretical standard deviation, and a judgment can be made about whether the dispersion in team standings is random or not. If clubs have equal playing strengths, then the probability of winning any one game is .5. If a club plays g games per season, the theoretical standard deviation of the win percent of the club over the season is $.5/\sqrt{g}$. For baseball, basketball (hockey), and football, these theoretical standard deviations are .039, .055, and .125, respectively. With equality of playing strengths among clubs, the theoretical standard deviations of the win percent in the leagues would also have these values.

Historical differences in the average win percent of clubs are mainly related to the size of the franchise market. The relationship between franchise market size and the average win percent is straightforward.[3] The marginal revenue product of a win is higher for a franchise located in a large city than for one located in a small city. This being so, a big-city club will tend to invest in a higher level of playing talent and win more games. Quirk and Fort have shown that the actual standard deviation of the win percent for league sports, on average, is about twice the theoretical standard deviation.[4] We can infer that if true competitive balance were present in leagues, the dispersion in club standings would be about half of that observed.

But this year-to-year dispersion in club standings within leagues is static, and it is only one source of the variance. There is nonrandom dispersion in the win percent for each and every club through time that is due to momentum, or serial correlation, in each club's win percent. Such dispersion is the focus of this chapter.

Table 4.1 presents calculations of the average win percent, the standard deviation of the win percent, and the coefficient of variation for the oldest clubs in baseball, basketball, and football. The measures for the leagues are across teams; the measures for the clubs are across time. Inspection of the table reveals that the variance in the win percent of clubs through time is about as large as the variance in the win percent within leagues. I calculated the theoretical variance of the win percent for each club. Dividing the observed standard deviation by the theoretical standard deviation, I found an average ratio of 1.9 in baseball, 2.0 in basketball, and 1.4 in football. Thus the observed dispersion of club performance is much larger than one would expect. Why? I will argue below that the pattern in the win percent of clubs through time does not exhibit random fluctuations around its mean win percent; rather, the pattern is one in which clubs exhibit momentum that leads to long cycles in their win records. A club develops a roster of playing talent, and as that playing talent matures, the club's fortune on the playing field improves relative to that of other clubs. Club performance reaches a peak, and then a period of serial decline sets in. About half or so of the variance in a club's win percent over time is due to this cycle of momentum.

The fact that there is nonrandom variance in a club's win percent over time has implications for the conclusion about the degree of inequality of playing strengths within leagues. The variance in the win percent is composed of the variance across clubs and among clubs through time. The ratio of the actual to the theoretical standard deviation across clubs is roughly 2, and within clubs through time it is also roughly 2, and there is no reason to believe that there is covariance between them. Thus about half of the variance attributed

Table 4.1 Measures of Historical Dispersion in Club Standings

Club	Mean	σ	σ/Mean
National League	.500	.086	.172
San Francisco Giants	.541	.076	.140
Los Angeles Dodgers	.523	.080	.147
Pittsburgh Pirates	.521	.085	.164
St. Louis Cardinals	.517	.085	.164
Chicago Cubs	.509	.085	.168
Cincinnati Reds	.505	.077	.152
Atlanta Braves	.463	.084	.182
Philadelphia Phils	.455	.090	.199
American League	.500	.089	.178
New York Yankees	.567	.082	.146
Detroit Tigers	.518	.069	.132
Boston Red Sox	.510	.087	.170
Cleveland Indians	.509	.068	.134
Chicago White Sox	.501	.075	.150
Oakland Athletics	.477	.115	.241
Baltimore Orioles	.475	.096	.202
Texas Rangers	.460	.083	.180
NBA	.500	.138	.276
Boston Celtics	.649	.126	.194
Los Angeles Lakers	.610	.131	.214
New York Knicks	.491	.127	.265
Golden State Warriors	.477	.123	.257
Detroit Pistons	.475	.123	.258
Sacramento Kings	.468	.116	.248
NFL	.500	.232	.464
Chicago Bears	.622	.210	.338
Green Bay Packers	.559	.218	.391
New York Giants	.556	.222	.400
Washington Redskins	.544	.200	.367
Detroit Lions	.486	.195	.401
Philadelphia Eagles	.437	.216	.494

to lack of competitive balance is really due to serial correlation or momentum. It is one thing to say that a league is unbalanced because the probability that the Yankees will win a game is .567, and for the Oakland Athletics it is .477. It is quite another to say that while, on average, the Yankees are better than the A's in any given season, depending on where the clubs are in their momentum cycle, the Oakland Athletics may be on top and the Yankees on the bottom.

The Time Profile of Playing Talent and Club Standing

Obviously the goal in a contest is to beat the opponent. In team sports this is accomplished by scoring more points or runs than the opponent. The win percentage of a club, W_t, is mainly determined by the stock of playing skills (offensive and defensive) of the team relative to that of the opponents in the league. Define club i's relative playing talent as $(T^{*i})_t = [T_i/n - i)]_t$, where T^i is the ith club's stock of playing talent, and $T/n - i$ is the mean stock of playing talent of the rest of the clubs in the league. Thus

$$W_t^i = f(T^{*i})_t. \tag{4.1}$$

At time t the stock of relative playing strength is the sum of an initial stock, $(T^{*i})_0$, and net changes in that stock.

$$(T^{*i})_t = (T^{*i})_0 + \Sigma_t \, \Delta(T^{*i})_t. \tag{4.2}$$

The change in a club's stock of playing skill is positive for replacement players whose skill is superior to that of the players replaced, and for retained players whose skills have improved. Playing skills tend to follow a career profile that rises over the early phase of a career and declines in the later phase. For some players on the roster (mainly starting veterans), skills eventually depreciate. I can illustrate this pattern with the careers of four great players: Hank Aaron, Reggie Jackson, Stan Musial, and Carl Yastrzemski. Figure 4.1 plots their season at bats relative to their average season at bats. Figure 4.2 plots their season slugging averages (SA) relative to their lifetime slugging averages. Both measures exhibit a nonlinear pattern. For the first fifteen years or so, their career at bats are above their historical averages. Then a decline in their appearance at the

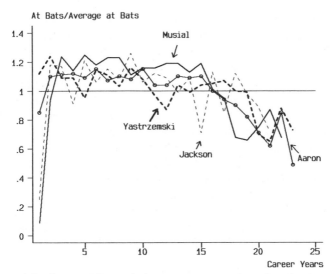

Figure 4.1   Season at bats relative to average season at bats for the careers of four baseball players.

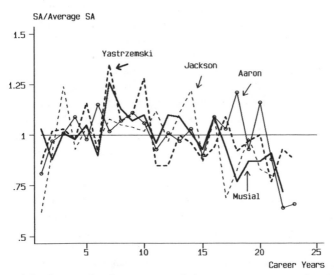

Figure 4.2   Season slugging average relative to average season slugging average for the careers of four baseball players.

plate sets in and is precipitous in the last few years of their careers. Their slugging averages tend to be above their historical averages in the roughly seven-to-ten-year period and then decline noticeably toward the end of their careers. Players like these stars and other lesser greats are kept on the roster at some sacrifice to the club win percent because fans come to see them play. Because roster size is fixed, the retention of aging veterans whose skills are in decline retards replacing vintage talent with new talent of similar skill. Each new addition to the roster has only a small probability of having a performance level equal to that of the fading stars on the roster. It may take a decade or longer to find a new Musial or Jackson.

Thus the path of a club's stock of playing talent over time is due to the increment of playing skill obtained through player replacement, ΔG_t, which may be negative, minus (plus) the depreciation (appreciation) of the skills of the veteran players, $(D^*)_t$.

$$(\Delta T^{*i})_t = (\Delta G^{*i})_t - (D^{*i})_t. \tag{4.3}$$

The Pattern of Club Standings

What is the likely pattern of the relative stock of playing talent on any particular club? If club management had perfect knowledge about playing skills, and if players were valued solely for skill, the relative stock of playing talent would fluctuate randomly around the profit-maximizing level of playing skill (win percent). As stated, the profit-maximizing win percent is mainly determined by the franchise market size of the club. It is more probable, however, that knowledge about playing skill is imperfect, that the parameters of a player's career profile are measured with error, and that aging veterans with declining playing skills draw fans for reasons beyond their contribution to team victories, which causes the stock of playing talent and hence the win percent to behave serially.

There are reasons beyond the pattern in the stock of playing skills that may be sources of cycles in the win percent of a club. Some clubs may invest in a level of playing skill that is above the profit-maximizing level. In this case the marginal cost of the win percent exceeds its marginal revenue. Such clubs may have to liquidate talented players to bring their player costs more in line with the revenue produced. The Oakland Athletics come to mind as an example. It is widely believed that the area around San Francisco, Oakland, and San Jose does not have a large enough population base to support two franchises. The failure of the Giants to acquire a new park at taxpayer expense in San Francisco or San Jose led to an offer by investors to move the club to St. Petersburg. The owners of the other clubs ultimately accepted the offer of San Francisco-based investors that kept the club in the city. Despite championship-caliber performance during the early 1970s, Oakland drew poorly. The club accumulated five divisional titles, three pennants, and three World Series from 1971 to 1975. Failing to find a buyer for the club, Charles O. Finley began selling off his talented players in 1976 (Joe Rudi, Rollie Fingers, and Vida Blue for $3.5 million). The liquidation of talent was so extreme that Commissioner Bowie Kuhn enjoined it as "inconsistent with the best interests of Baseball, the integrity of the game and public confidence in it." In the late 1980s the Athletics again were a powerhouse, winning three pennants (1988–90) and a World Series. The club drew 2.9 million fans in 1990, about 700,000 above the baseball average. But Toronto and Los Angeles, both with modest seasons (.531 win percents), respectively drew 3.9 and 3.0 million fans. Average player salary in Oakland for the 1991 season was $1.35 million, the highest in baseball. With attendance about a third above the baseball average, but player pay more than 50 percent above the average, Oakland's level of playing talent may not be sustainable in the 1990s, as was true in the 1970s—and many crossover fans have been drawn to watch Barry Bonds play across the bay. Thus cycles in the win percent may be partly due to adjustments in team quality to yield the long-run, profit-maximizing, equilibrium win percent.

Significant changes in playing rules may bring about cycles in the win percent. The introduction of the lively ball into baseball and the banning of the spitball and scuffball in 1920, changes in the strike zone, the imposition of uniform fence distances, and so on may have altered the productivity of playing assets differently across clubs. It may have taken several seasons to make adjustments. The forward pass, changes in the hash marks, and so on in football, and the twenty-four-second clock and the three-point shot in basketball are further examples of rule changes that may have altered the productivity of playing skills differently across clubs.

A pattern of rising player quality (win percent) on a club followed by a decline is known as *momentum* in sports, or *serial correlation* in time series analysis. Momentum, or serial correlation, means that current values (residuals) are determined by past values (residuals).

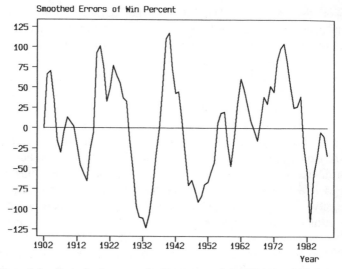

Figure 4.3   Smoothed errors of win percent of the Cincinnati Reds, 1902–88.

The momentum pattern in the win percents of clubs in professional sports is shown in the pattern of the smoothed residuals of the Cincinnati Reds, Green Bay Packers, and New York Knicks in figures 4.3–4.5.

Consider in figure 4.6 the serial pattern in the relative stock of playing talent of the Cincinnati Reds over the period 1901–89. Cincinnati's offensive (hitting) skill is its runs produced against other clubs during the season divided by the average number of runs produced by the other clubs in the league. Cincinnati's defensive (pitching) skill is the league average (less Cincinnati) of the runs scored against teams divided by the runs scored against Cincinnati. The data are detrended; hence the measures are the residuals in each series. To remove annual (noise) fluctuations, the residuals are smoothed by a three-year moving average. A definite cyclical pattern (momentum) is obvious in both series.

Two statistical procedures can be utilized to assess the pattern of serial correlation: distributed lags or the Box-Jenkins (ARMA) model. In the context of a dependent variable that is statistically determined by past values of that variable, the distributed lag model

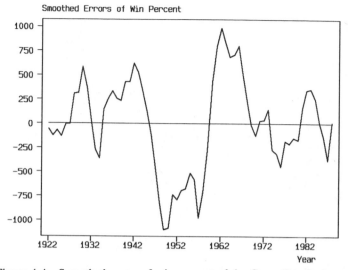

Figure 4.4   Smoothed errors of win percent of the Green Bay Packers, 1922–88.

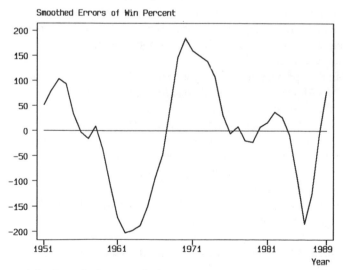

Figure 4.5   Smoothed errors of win percent of the New York Knicks, 1951–89.

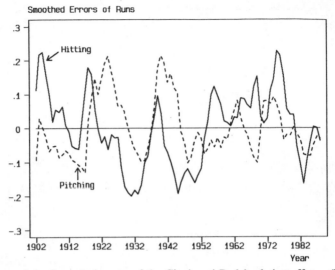

Figure 4.6   Smoothed errors of the Cincinnati Reds' relative offense (hitting) and defense (pitching) against National League clubs, 1902–88.

is a subset of the Box-Jenkins model. Thus the ARMA procedure is employed here. In the Box-Jenkins model, autocorrelation coefficients of various lag lengths are obtained. Because the data have been detrended and smoothed, only the autoregressive part of the model is estimated.

In the appendix to this chapter, table 4A.1 presents the autocorrelation (AR) coefficients of the residuals of Cincinnati's relative runs and the relative runs scored by opponents. The model is an adequate representation of the pattern in the residuals, judged by the adjusted coefficients of determination and the low standard errors. The values of the residuals lagged one year are positively correlated with the current-period residuals; the lags at two and three years are negatively correlated, at four years positively correlated, at five and six years negatively correlated, at seven years positively correlated, and at eight years negatively correlated.

Empirical Evidence on Momentum in Team Win Percents

For all of the data series employed here, the residuals were obtained from a simple detrending procedure, and annual randomness was removed by a three-year moving average on the residuals. I experimented with moving averages of a longer period, but they added no efficiency.[5]

Box-Jenkins estimation is a purely empirical procedure. Autocorrelations were specified of 1–20 years in length. The criteria for selecting the appropriate lag length were the standard error of the estimate, the adjusted coefficient of determination, and the Durbin-Watson statistic.[6]

Baseball

Only the clubs with the longest historical records were selected; hence there were eight clubs each in the National League and the American League over the period 1901–89. The autocorrelations for the National League appear in table 4A.2, while those of the American League teams appear in table 4A.3. The most frequent number of autocorrelations was eight. There were six cases of five-year autocorrelations and three cases of seven-year autocorrelations. The adjusted R^2's averaged 0.86 and ranged between 0.74 and 0.91. The standard errors of the estimate averaged 23.5 and ranged between 21.6 and 29.3. The explanatory power of the autoregressive model is quite good.

The sign pattern in the autocorrelation coefficients shows a strong cyclical pattern in the data. This is also true for the data on NFL and NBA clubs that follow. The values lagged one year are always positively correlated with the current values of the residual. The values lagged two and three years are always negatively correlated with the current value of the residuals. The values lagged four years are always (except for the Knicks in the NBA) positively correlated with the current values. The values lagged six and eight years are nearly always correlated negatively, and at seven years they are positively correlated.

Football

Only clubs with the longest data records in the NFL were selected: the Green Bay Packers (1921–89), the Chicago Bears (from 1922), the New York Giants (from 1925), Philadelphia (from 1933), Detroit (from 1934), and Washington (from 1937). The autocorrelations appear in appendix table 4A.4. The adjusted R^2's averaged 0.78 and ranged between 0.67 and 0.86. The average value of the standard errors was 187.9 and ranged from 90.0 to 247.0. The number of games played in a season of football is a small fraction of the games played in baseball. The greater variance in the win percents is therefore hardly surprising. The sign pattern of the autocorrelation coefficients follows that of baseball.

Basketball

There were continuous data from 1950 to 1990 for six NBA teams. The autocorrelations appear in appendix table 4A.5. Three teams had autocorrelations of five years, one team had four years, one had seven years, and one had eight years. The average value of the adjusted R^2's was 0.81 and ranged between 0.64 and 0.90. The average value of the standard errors was 36.9 and ranged between 30.3 and 44.3. There are about one-half the number of games in an NBA season as in a baseball season. The sign pattern of the autocorrelation coefficients is similar to the patterns for baseball and football.

Implication: Fans Need to Be Patient

One implication of this analysis is that more is required than changing the manager or adding new playing talent to bring a club from middling to championship caliber. Clearly, better players and coaches matter. In rare instances, as in baseball under free agency, a club can buy wisely in the market for experienced veteran talent and immediately propel itself to a championship; recall, for example, the remarkable transformation of Atlanta and Minnesota, which both finished last in their divisions in the 1990 season; then finished division winners and league champions in the 1991 season. The acquisition of Barry Bonds by the San Francisco Giants has led to a remarkable turnaround for the club. The Dallas Cowboys had a dismal 1–15 record in 1989 and then crushed Buffalo in Super Bowl XXVII. But new talent and better management are only the necessary, not the sufficient, conditions for vastly improving the win percent of the team. Generally it takes time for talent to mature and for new players on the club to interact with one another to achieve the highest quality of play on the field.

Look again at figures 4.3–4.5. The average number of years between peak performances of the Cincinnati Reds is about ten years. The average years between troughs is about eleven years. For Green Bay the average from peak to peak is about eleven years, and from trough to trough it is about ten years. There are fewer peaks and troughs for the New York Knicks, so the averages are less reliable: eleven years from peak to peak and twelve years from trough to trough.

Is the Momentum Model More General Than in Sports?

Firms that sell some differentiated products may have a serial pattern in their market share similar to that in professional team sports, and for broadly similar reasons. For example, programming is a main determinant of a network's share of a television audience. Such programming involves scripts or events, actors, and other inputs. Audiences respond to these inputs differently, and the response may mimic the momentum or serial correlation in team sports.

This hypothesis is tested using the annual Nielsen ratings of CBS, NBC, and ABC from the 1952–53 to 1989–90 television seasons. The market share of each network is expressed as a fraction of the three network Nielsen ratings. As with the sports data, the share data was detrended and the errors smoothed with a three-year moving average. A cyclical pattern in the market share is illustrated for CBS-TV in figure 4.7. The Box-Jenkins autocorrelations appear in table 4A.6. The mean adjusted R^2 is 0.90, and the mean standard error is 0.56. Five years was the best empirical representation. The sign pattern of the autocorrelations is similar for all of the networks.

Some other industries, for example, the movie industry prior to the rise of television or the computer software industry, may also

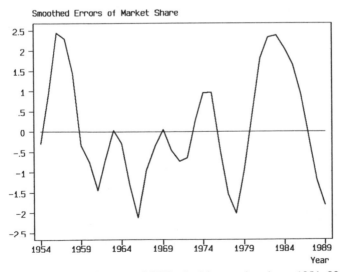

Figure 4.7   Smoothed errors of CBS television market share, 1954–89.

have this pattern of market share. During the era of the studio system, movie companies kept actors under contracts similar to the reserve-clause contracts used in baseball. Studio acting talent made films that competed with those made by the actors under contract with other studios. Movie stars have fans, but fans are fickle. The market shares of the movie studios might very well mimic the serial pattern shown in sports and television. In the software industry there is a product cycle of several years for programs. Innovation in software programs alters market share. Market shares in the automotive, soft drink, and beer industries might also exhibit a cyclic pattern.

Appendix to Chapter 4

Table 4A.1   Autocorrelations of Relative Playing Skills of the Cincinnati Reds, 1902–88

AR	Errors of Relative Runs Produced	Errors of Relative Opponent Runs
AR_{-1}	1.44	1.30
	(12.86)	(11.18)
AR_{-2}	$-.48$	$-.32$
	(2.54)	(1.68)
AR_{-3}	$-.53$	$-.56$
	(2.82)	(2.96)
AR_{-4}	.83	.80
	(4.36)	(4.17)
AR_{-5}	$-.45$	$-.47$
	(2.35)	(2.45)
AR_{-6}	$-.26$	$-.16$
	(1.34)	(0.83)
AR_{-7}	.63	.31
	(3.43)	(1.72)
AR_{-8}	$-.34$	$-.18$
	(3.15)	(1.65)
R^2 Adj.	.87	.86
DW	1.83	1.99
SEE	.038	.034

Table 4A.2   Autocorrelations of Errors of Win Percents of National League Teams, 1902–88

AR	Cards	Pirates	Phils	Giants	Reds	Cubs	Braves	Dodgers
AR_{-1}	1.23	1.33	1.45	1.21	1.30	1.42	1.42	1.43
	(11.66)	(11.93)	(13.03)	(10.72)	(11.53)	(12.05)	(12.31)	(12.28)
AR_{-2}	− .35	− .29	− .37	− .35	− .37	− .47	− .41	− .66
	(2.15)	(1.59)	(2.02)	(2.05)	(2.02)	(2.33)	(2.10)	(3.31)
AR_{-3}	− .35	− .56	− .58	− .45	− .56	− .84	− .79	− .32
	(2.05)	(2.97)	(3.42)	(2.63)	(3.03)	(4.08)	(4.00)	(1.70)
AR_{-4}	.63	.69	.59	.63	.74	1.23	1.03	.89
	(3.74)	(3.64)	(3.47)	(3.59)	(3.89)	(5.70)	(4.78)	(5.62)
AR_{-5}	− .27	− .13	− .22	− .24	− .21	− .42	− .32	− .84
	(2.48)	(0.70)	(2.14)	(1.35)	(1.08)	(1.91)	(1.52)	(4.34)
AR_{-6}		− .36		− .30	− .49	− .41	− .38	.42
		(1.89)		(1.80)	(2.35)	(1.91)	(1.92)	(2.10)
AR_{-7}		.18		.47	.60	.53	.53	− .06
		(1.53)		(2.90)	(2.97)	(2.62)	(2.71)	(0.52)
AR_{-8}				− .29	− .36	− .24	− .25	
				(2.86)	(3.09)	(2.14)	(2.14)	
R^2 Adj.	.87	.88	.91	.74	.86	.83	.84	.83
DW	2.01	1.93	2.00	2.02	1.94	1.96	1.86	1.99
SEE	23.14	23.32	23.50	21.55	22.64	21.84	25.61	21.77

Table 4A.3   Autocorrelations of Errors of Win Percents of American League Teams, 1902–88

AR	Yankees	Red Sox	White Sox	Indians	Tigers	Orioles	Athletics	Rangers
AR_{-1}	1.47	1.25	1.23	1.24	1.30	1.49	1.57	1.28
	(13.60)	(11.27)	(10.99)	(11.60)	(12.30)	(14.63)	(14.05)	(11.00)
AR_{-2}	− .72	− .03	− .08	− .07	− .53	− .46	− .75	− .12
	(3.93)	(0.18)	(0.49)	(0.45)	(3.33)	(2.77)	(3.68)	(0.64)
AR_{-3}	− .19	− .76	− .72	− .87	− .48	− .72	− .19	− .85
	(0.94)	(4.67)	(5.13)	(5.21)	(3.19)	(4.93)	(0.88)	(4.90)
AR_{-4}	.63	.76	.57	.77	.71	.98	.60	.52
	(3.44)	(4.17)	(3.45)	(4.41)	(4.68)	(6.38)	(3.03)	(2.60)
AR_{-5}	− .29	− .22	− .18	− .07	− .40	− .44	− .45	.30
	(2.69)	(1.23)	(1.63)	(0.38)	(3.92)	(4.36)	(2.32)	(1.51)
AR_{-6}		− .44		− .64			− .21	− .46
		(2.75)		(3.75)			(1.03)	(2.66)

Table 4A.3   (*continued*)

AR	Yankees	Red Sox	White Sox	Indians	Tigers	Orioles	Athletics	Rangers
AR_{-7}		.57		.36			.56	.27
		(3.50)		(3.31)			(2.91)	(1.44)
AR_{-8}		−.29					−.33	−.07
		(3.04)					(3.07)	(0.66)
R^2 Adj.	.88	.91	.82	.83	.77	.89	.91	.83
DW	1.97	1.92	1.98	1.95	1.96	1.94	1.88	1.96
SEE	23.36	21.67	24.58	21.48	22.95	23.91	29.26	24.67

Table 4A.4   Autocorrelations of Errors of Win Percents of National Football League Teams, 1922–88

AR	Packers	Bears	Giants	Phil.	Detroit	Wash.
AR_{-1}	1.37	1.20	1.06	1.57	1.18	1.25
	(9.61)	(9.21)	(7.19)	(10.44)	(7.72)	(7.89)
AR_{-2}	−.32	−.17	−.03	−1.04	−.33	−.09
	(1.33)	(0.91)	(0.12)	(3.82)	(1.45)	(0.38)
AR_{-3}	−.74	−.84	−.79	−.07	−.67	−.67
	(3.24)	(4.80)	(4.05)	(0.25)	(3.05)	(2.67)
AR_{-4}	.78	.87	.69	.56	.90	.44
	(3.10)	(4.21)	(2.86)	(1.89)	(3.77)	(1.65)
AR_{-5}	−.04	−.23	.01	.01	−.37	.16
	(0.15)	(1.13)	(0.04)	(0.05)	(1.54)	(0.67)
AR_{-6}	−.53	−.40	−.44	−.68	−.34	−.51
	(2.33)	(2.32)	(2.24)	(2.37)	(1.50)	(1.99)
AR_{-7}	.49	.73	.35	.70	.60	.29
	(2.08)	(4.04)	(1.64)	(2.63)	(2.69)	(1.79)
AR_{-8}	−.25	−.40	−.16	−.37	−.29	
	(1.74)	(2.96)	(1.02)	(2.44)	(2.02)	
R^2 Adj.	.86	.77	.67	.83	.71	.83
DW	1.90	2.08	2.01	1.84	2.05	1.91
SEE	89.97	198.82	247.03	198.33	208.14	184.98

Table 4A.5   Autocorrelations of Errors of Win Percents of National Basketball
Association Teams, 1951–89

AR	Knicks	G. State	Celtics	Lakers	Kings	Pistons
AR₋₁	1.82	1.11	1.51	1.38	1.25	1.54
	(10.53)	(6.17)	(7.97)	(7.54)	(8.55)	(8.77)
AR₋₂	−1.48	−.11	−.67	−.73	−.35	−.71
	(4.25)	(0.53)	(1.94)	(2.36)	(1.60)	(2.27)
AR₋₃	.77	−.52	−.82	−.19	−.59	−.28
	(2.15)	(2.64)	(2.22)	(0.61)	(2.96)	(0.83)
AR₋₄	−.30	.61	1.40	.70	.86	.58
	(1.61)	(2.88)	(3.72)	(2.49)	(4.07)	(1.83)
AR₋₅		−.28	−.83	−.68	−.56	−.33
		(1.78)	(2.18)	(2.21)	(4.00)	(1.84)
AR₋₆			−.25	.22		
			(0.63)	(0.72)		
AR₋₇			.70	.05		
			(2.04)	(0.26)		
AR₋₈			−.39			
			(2.15)			
R^2 Adj.	.90	.64	.83	.79	.86	.85
DW	2.02	2.16	1.89	1.95	2.00	2.04
SEE	33.77	44.26	40.49	36.62	30.33	35.59

Table 4A.6   Autocorrelations of Errors of Market Shares of
Network Television, 1954–1989

AR	CBS-TV	NBC-TV	ABC-TV
AR₋₁	1.55	1.49	1.87
	(8.95)	(8.41)	(11.03)
AR₋₂	−.76	−.36	−1.29
	(2.65)	(1.15)	(3.42)
AR₋₃	−.60	−.61	−.07
	(2.09)	(2.01)	(0.14)
AR₋₄	.95	.60	.81
	(3.45)	(2.08)	(2.09)
AR₋₅	−.47	−.33	−.50
	(2.86)	(2.00)	(2.91)
R^2 Adj.	.85	.93	.93
DW	2.11	1.83	2.09
SEE	.50	.59	.59

△

△

△ **F I V E**

▼ Reputational Capital and the
Sale of Franchises
▼

▼ Reputational Capital and the
Sale of Franchises
▼

Introduction

In theory the sales price of a going enterprise is the cost of replicating
its assets. A buyer will pay no more than it would cost to start a
comparable enterprise from scratch. A seller will take no less than
the market value of the assets. Yet firms have reputations as well
as assets, and business reputations may be good or bad. The most
obvious instances of a bad reputation are bankruptcy and managerial
ineptitude that leads to poor returns on assets. Firms with poor reputations sell at prices below the cost of replicating the assets, and
have a higher probability of being sold, because new owners with
average business skills can earn at least the competitive return on
the assets. Some firms have good reputations, and they may sell at
prices greater than the cost of replicating their assets. The theory of
why reputable firms exchange at a price above the cost of replicating
their assets is not well developed. One possibility is that reputable
firms have a larger market share (sales per unit of assets) and more
loyal (repeat) customers than firms with average or poor reputations.
Another argument rests on the notion of the "winner's curse." In
an auction the winner (the one paying the highest price for the asset)
is the person with the greatest expectation of making a return on
the investment. The notion of the winner's curse arose out of the
observations on bids and returns for leases on oil-producing properties. All bidders had similar geological information on the prospects

for oil. Winners of the leases paid more than the expected value of the petroleum, and hence were losers.

Sports provide a good opportunity for modeling and measuring the effect of reputation. I showed that teams do not have win percents (outputs) that randomly fluctuate around the mean; rather, they have long cycles of momentum. Over some period, a club's record improves serially, perhaps culminating in a championship. This is followed by a period of serial decline, perhaps culminating in a cellar finish. Over this momentum cycle teams acquire reputations as winners or losers. Reputation affects the value and the timing of the sale of sport franchises.

Although it is dangerous to make generalizations from specific cases, let me give an example anyway. A full analysis of all franchise sales follows, so the example will do no harm to the evidence. Consider the Boston Celtics, a club with an extraordinarily good reputation in the last decade or so, and the Denver Nuggets, a team recognized as mediocre at best and poor at worst. In 1983 Harry Mangurian sold the Celtics for $15 million to Allen Cohen, Don Gaston, and Paul DuPee. In 1986 the club offered 2.6 million shares (a 40-percent stake) to the public at $18.50 a share, making the implicit value of the club $120 million. The capital appreciation rate of the Celtics over the period 1983–86 was a whopping 200 percent per year. *Financial World* estimated the 1991 value of the club at $180 million.[1] When Mangurian sold the club, the Celtics had a win percent of .756 and were the world champions. In 1981–82 its record was .768 percent, but the club lost to Philadelphia (4–3) in the play-offs. In 1982–83 its record was .683 percent, and the club lost early on in the play-offs (decisively to the Bucks, 4–0). Under Cohen, Gaston, and DuPee, its record was .756 (1983–84), .768 (1984–85), .817 (1985–86), .729 (1986–87), .695 (1987–88), .512 (1988–89), and .646 (1989–90). The Celtics were world champions in 1984 and 1986, and consistently made the play-offs.

Red McCombs sold the Denver Nuggets to Sidney Schlenker and Allen Becker for $19 million in 1985. The club had a checkered record for a few years before the sale: .549 (1982–83), .463 (1983–84), and .634 (1984–85). In 1989 the Nuggets were sold for $54 million to Bertram Lee, Peter Bynoe, and Robert Wussler. The annual capital appreciation rate of the Nuggets over the period 1985–89 was 29.8 percent. *Financial World* estimated that the 1991 value of the club had dropped to $40.6 million. The poor financial performance of the Nuggets relative to the Celtics may be due to its reputation as a mediocre club and its sliding into a loser status. Its record on the court indicates that this is so: .573 (1985–86), .451 (1986–87), .659 (1987–88), .537 (1988–89), .524 (1989–90), .244 (1990–91), and .293 (1991–92).[2]

Reputations and Asset Values

In equilibrium the value of assets employed in productive activity is their value in their next best alternative employment. Because all assets in competitive equilibrium earn their opportunity cost, they exchange at a price that in their new employment will earn the competitive return over their remaining useful economic lives. Some assets of a firm may be specific or peculiar to their particular employments. Specific assets earn the competitive rate of return in their particular employments, but exchange at a discount. The competitive discount on the sale of specific assets is determined by their value in an alternative employment. For example, a machine tool that produces a specific output peculiar to a firm will exchange at less than the price of a general machine tool. The equilibrium price differential will be the cost of converting the specific machine tool into one that is suitable for its alternative employment.

Intangible assets may be general or specific. A customer list or a distribution network are general intangible assets that exchange at the opportunity cost of replicating them. Brand names, trademarks, and business reputations are specific intangible assets whose value is peculiar to the firm. Akerlof and Klein and Leffler have identified product brand name and guarantee, firm logo, advertising, product endorsements, franchising and chaining, and licensing as nonprice, firm-specific investments that are undertaken to signal product quality to consumers.[3] Such investments are like physical investments and are capitalized in the value of the firm. Beyond these tangible and intangible assets, firms may have good or bad reputations.[4] These intangible assets are reputational capital that affect the exchange price of physical capital (both general and specific).

Bankruptcy is bad reputation. It has been observed that the assets of bankrupt firms exchange at a lower price than those of nonbankrupt firms, and that the prices of foreclosed houses or commercial property and automobiles are lower than the prices of nonforeclosed assets. In the case of bankrupt firms, part of the price differential may be due to thinness of the market and urgency to sell to satisfy creditors. In the case of foreclosed, mortgaged property, part of the price differential may be due to urgency of the bank to recover as much of the loan as possible as quickly as possible, an unwillingness of the bank to undertake another line of business (e.g., sale of previously owned property), and discounts to middlemen to unload bank property quickly. Part of the price differential, however, may be due to bad reputation. In the case of repossessed automobiles, buyers may believe that the automobile was abused or not maintained. In the case of bankrupt firms, particularly those that rely on repeat business, there may be a perception of unreliability and potential malfeasance (cost-cutting during start-up by the new owner) that results in previous customers switching their business to competing firms. The bad reputational capital of bankrupt firms implies that the physical assets of such firms will exchange at lower prices than their replication cost for reasons beyond thinness of the market or creditor pressure.

Some firms have good reputations. These firms make products or provide services that are perceived by customers to be of particularly high quality. Where product or service quality is due entirely to capital (physical and human) investment, assets of high-quality firms exchange at their replication cost, no more and no less. In equilibrium the increased cost of production is reflected in a price differential for the product or service. Where price differentials do not exist for products or services that differ by quality, pure reputational rents (positive or negative) are earned by firms. For example, in Dallas most automobile-dealer repair shops charge $40 per hour for labor, and parts prices are uniform. Quality of repair varies across dealers. Dealers with good service reputations sell more cars, perhaps at higher average prices, and retain customers. Dealers with poor service reputations sell fewer cars, and retain fewer repeat customers. Over time, automobile dealerships establish good and bad reputations. At the point of sale of their assets, dealerships with good reputations will exchange at a higher price than dealerships with bad reputations. The prospective new owner has some assurance that customers will continue to deal with the firm with an established reputation for quality. This stream of net revenue from customer satisfaction is capitalized in the exchange price of the franchise. The argument, *mutatis mutandis,* holds for firms with bad reputations. The bad reputation (negative rents) is capitalized in the exchange value of the assets.

To continue with examples from the automobile market, consider the effect on General Motors and Ford of two inglorious cars. The Chevrolet Corvair was introduced in September, 1959. Sales were brisk for the aluminum, air-cooled, rear-engine automobile. From 1960 through 1963 all Corvairs had swing-axle suspension; coupled with a rear engine, this gave the car a marked propensity to oversteer. To improve steering control, a traverse leaf spring was installed in the rear and an antisway bar in the front of the 1964 model. In 1965 a link-type suspension with dual control arms replaced the swing-axle suspension. The redesigned rear suspension reduced the tuck-under hazard of the Corvair.

In 1965 Ralph Nader made his reputation with *Unsafe at Any Speed,* a book that killed the Corvair. Accusing GM of great industrial irresponsibility in producing the car from 1960 to 1963 with the swing-axle design, he documented the steering and control problems of the Corvair. Sales of the Corvair were 196,000 units in 1964. After the publication of the book sales plummeted; sales of the 1966 model were 73,000 units. The reputation of the Corvair hurt Chevrolet. In 1963 Chevrolet had a 30.1-percent share of the domestic market compared to Ford's 21.4 percent. In 1966 Chevrolet's share was 25.6 percent compared to Ford's 28.2 percent. The last Corvair was produced for the 1969 model year. General Motors may be entering another period of poor reputation because of the design of its pickup trucks built from the mid-70s to mid-80s. These vehicles had the gas tank(s) mounted outside of the frame, which gave them a tendency to burst into flames in side collisions. As with the Corvair, liability suits are proliferating.

The Ford Pinto weighed less than 2,000 pounds, cost $2,000, and was designed to compete with the small-car imports. Sales of the car were brisk after it was first introduced in September, 1970. The 1971–76 models had a tendency to explode on impact after relatively low speed, rear-end collisions. In the fall of 1977, *Mother Jones* magazine broke an investigative story about the Ford Pinto. Sales of the car fell dramatically, and the public perceived that Ford automobiles were unsafe.[5] In 1974 Ford had a 23.4-percent share of the domestic market, while Chevrolet had 26.0 percent. In 1979 Ford's share was 16.4 percent compared to Chevrolet's share of 26.5 percent. Ford installed a polyethylene shield to prevent puncturing of the gas tank in the 1977 model. Production of the car ceased with the 1980 model.

Examples abound in other markets as well. Food Lion supermarkets were charged with selling tainted meat in 1992. Sales plummeted. The outbreak of bacterial food poisoning at Jack-in-the-Box franchises in the Northwest led to some deaths of small children and a serious loss of business in early 1993. Bill padding and charge for work never done at Sears Auto Centers harmed the reputation of a company long known for reliable treatment of its customers. Word-Perfect and WordStar compete in the market for word processors, and both programs are upgraded occasionally. The upgrades for WordPerfect have been compatible with earlier versions, making for trouble-free adaptation by users; WordStar upgrades have not been compatible. WordPerfect offers a toll-free number for users; Word-Star does not. WordPerfect is a billion-dollar enterprise; the stock of WordStar is worth $63 million. In the 1960s Schlitz beer was second in sales in America. To cut costs, Schlitz replaced barley malt with corn syrup and cut fermentation time drastically. Sales fell 90 percent.[6]

Reputations and the Value and Timing of the Sale of Franchises

Figure 5.1a shows the equilibrium win percent and ticket price for a hypothetical club. All teams face the same supply function of player talent. While other inputs are used to produce wins (e.g., managers, coaches), the principal factor in club standing is player talent. While the relationship between club win percent and team inputs is well known, for the sake of completeness I discuss the evidence. A linear regression of 1988 team win percent on 1988 values of the team slugging average (a measure of hitting), the team earned-run average (a measure of pitching quality), and an American League dummy (to capture the effect of the designated-hitter rule), yielded the following results. Each .001-point increase in the team slugging average added .0015 to the team win percent. Each .01-point increase in the team ERA reduced the team win percent by .0015.[7] The R^2 was .80.

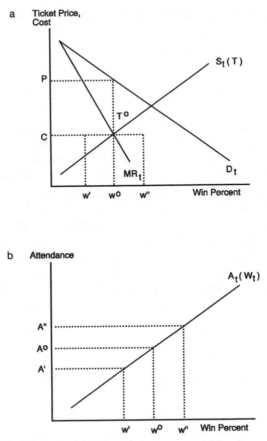

Figure 5.1   Theoretical relationship between a club's win percent and ticket price, attendance, profit, and value of the franchise.

Other costs, such as stadium rental, travel, game, and administrative costs, can be treated as fixed and independent of the team's win percent. The demand for wins depends on the size of the franchise market, which is measured conventionally by SMSA or MSA population, and on the elasticity of demand for winning, which includes such factors as per capita income and number of competing sports.[8] Evidence suggests that clubs set ticket prices at the point where the elasticity of demand is unity.[9] Of course these parameters set the scale and the slope of the demand curve. Differences across clubs in

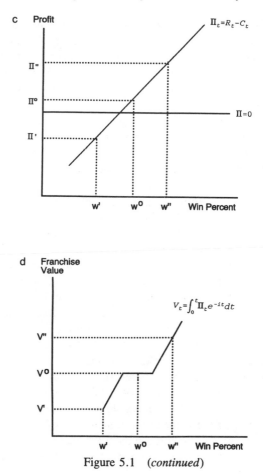

Figure 5.1 (*continued*)

the level or elasticity of demand for winning correspond to historical differences in club standing. Conventionally, clubs in big cities or with fickle fans win more games than small-city clubs or clubs with loyal fans.[10]

The hypothetical club depicted in the figure has a profit-maximizing win percent of $w°$. The profit-maximizing level of player talent is $T°$. Of course clubs are not always successful in transforming the profit-maximizing level of talent into the profit-maximizing win percent. The theoretical standard deviation of the win percent in baseball is $.500/\sqrt{162} = .039$. Thus for purely statistical reasons, or reasons of fortune, an average club, at one standard deviation, may fall in the win percent interval of .461–.539. Over time, however, as discussed in the previous chapter, clubs may have much larger deviations from the profit-maximizing win percent than the theoretical deviation. For example, the Atlanta Braves, National League champions for the 1991 season, through 1989 had a record as good as .617 (1957) and as poor as .248 (1935) percent. The standard deviation of the win percent for the club is .084 percent, which is 2.2 times the theoretical standard deviation.

Thus a club with a profit-maximizing level of playing talent may produce a level of victories within a fairly wide range. The range of win percent for the talent level $T°$ of the hypothetical team at time t in the figure is $w' - w''$. Over this range of club victories, player costs are invariant, but attendance is strictly related to the win percent. For victories over the range $w' - w''$, attendance will vary from A' to A'', as shown in figure 5.1b. Because revenue is proportional to the club win percent, but costs are fixed, club profits are positive for win percent near $w°$ and above, and are low or negative for win percents at some level below $w°$ (see fig. 5.1c).

The value of a franchise is the discounted net cash flow of the club. Over some range in the win percent, say $\lambda\sigma_w$, the value of a franchise is a constant. The value of λ is an empirical matter. In other words good and bad luck, as random events, do not affect the market perception of the value of the franchise. However if the club win percent is, say, two or three standard deviations from $w°$, and if this is not a random event, the market value of the franchise is affected. A club that is sustaining a record of say two or three standard deviations above $w°$ is perceived as a winner (good reputation), while a club that is sustaining a record of two or three standard deviations below $w°$ is perceived as a loser (bad reputation). These reputational effects are theorized to affect the price at which the franchise will exchange (see fig. 5.1d).

The variable that is utilized in the statistical analysis of franchise sales is the number of games behind the leader. It is worth the trouble to show the relationship between games behind and attendance. Figure 5.2 plots the number of games out of first place, and figure 5.3 the attendance of the Atlanta Braves for the period

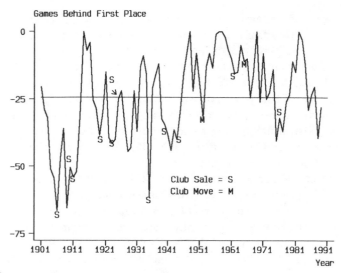

Figure 5.2   Games out of first place of the Atlanta Braves, 1901–89.

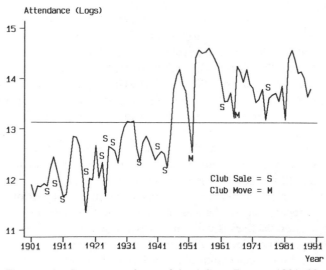

Figure 5.3   Season attendance of the Atlanta Braves, 1901–89.

1901–89. The games-behind variable has been entered as a negative number to facilitate comparison with attendance. Attendance is in logs for better resolution in the graph. Both variables contain statistically significant trends. On average, the club was better after World War II, and the better attendance in part explains the scalar shift in attendance. Clearly, attendance and club performance are related, just by visual inspection. More formally, the simple correlation between, first, differences in games behind (measured now as a positive number) and fan attendance is − .46. Alternatively, in a regression of attendance on games behind and trend, the regression coefficient of games behind is − 15,858, and it is highly significant.[11] Thus, on average, an extra game behind the leader is associated with a loss of about 16,000 fans for the Atlanta Braves.

There is a second noteworthy feature of the figures. While the data are a little noisy, and this is expected, given our discussion of the role of luck (theoretical standard deviation of winning), there are clear long-term cycles in the win percent and attendance. The previous chapter showed that all clubs in all sports go through periods of rising performance and then periods of decline. In the case of the Atlanta Braves, with the data smoothed by a five-year moving average, there were five peaks and five troughs. The average time from peak to peak was sixteen years, and the average from trough to trough was fifteen years. In the previous chapter I theorized that a club's search for and development of playing talent takes considerable time. As players are developed, their skills and performance increase, and these net increments to the stock of club playing talent increase the win percent. Player skills reach a peak and then decline. Veteran star players attract fans for reasons beyond their playing skills (recognition and reputation). Because roster size is fixed, and aging veterans' skills are in decline, the retention of these star players leads to a decline in club standing. Eventually, the stars are replaced with rookies, and the club's fortunes on the playing field decline until the new rookie talent matures.

This momentum in club win percent mimics a pattern of good and bad reputation. As the team declines over a long period of time, its reputation declines. Losing in sports is equivalent to bankruptcy. A long pattern of decline and a level of decline that leads to severe financial distress can bankrupt a franchise and induce a distress sale. A number of clubs have been bankrupt or have been near bankruptcy

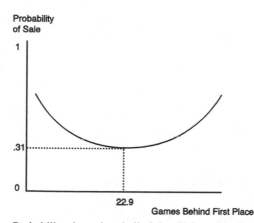

Figure 5.4   Probability that a baseball club will be sold related to games behind first place.

because of long stays in the cellar: the original Washington Senators (1903), the Braves while in Boston (1923, 1935), Cincinnati (1933, 1934), the Philadelphia Phils (1943), Kansas City (1960), Seattle (1970), and the Chicago Cubs (1981), among others. At the other extreme are clubs that have been sold at the peak of their playing quality. Clubs sold after league championships include the Boston Red Sox (four times between 1903 and 1916), the St. Louis Browns (1945), the New York Yankees (1964), and the Baltimore Orioles (1979), among others.

The above discussion suggests the pattern in the probability of a sale of a franchise shown in figure 5.4. Bankrupt or cellar teams are sold for reasons of financial distress. Because of a bad reputation, the club's assets exchange for less than the assets of a club in a market of similar size with an average reputation. There exists a market of specialists who believe that they can take over a club's playing assets and transform the bad reputation into an average reputation. The argument is similar to that in Manne's discussion of takeover or horizontal merger of assets.[12] Thus the probability of a sale is high for clubs with bad reputations.

Clubs with good reputations (e.g., those with positive momentum that culminates in a league championship) will exchange at a price above the price of a club in a market of similar size with an average reputation. Thus the probability of a sale also is high for franchises with good reputations. Because the evidence on momentum suggests that there are cycles in reputations, the payment of a premium for a winning franchise would seem irrational. Such sales are partly due to the "winner's curse" and partly to asymmetrical information between the buyer and seller. The buyer purchases the team for his own use, and he and other potential buyers have different estimates of their ability to run the team. As in a common-value auction, the winning bid is from the buyer with the highest regard for his abilities to run the club. Furthermore the information between the seller and the potential bidders may be asymmetric and not very dense. The seller is likely to know with more certainty than potential buyers the path of future team performance, given the stock of playing talent. Potential buyers may overestimate their ability to maintain the team's momentum with acquisitions in the players' market. In addition the presence of considerable noise around the long-term momentum cycles (recall figure 5.2) may mask the serial correlation. Furthermore, despite the fact that many teams have existed for ninety years or more, the number of cycles is small, and conditions may have changed to discount predictions of future performance on the basis of past performance (e.g., the role of national television revenue in socializing income among the clubs). A winner's curse has been observed in book publishing and in the market for free-agent players.[13] A winner's curse may operate in the market for movie stars and may also have arisen in the market for sports-broadcast rights. CBS-TV paid $1 billion for the NFL's right and $1.06 billion for baseball's rights. It has taken $604 million in pretax write-offs on the baseball contract because advertising revenues failed to cover the payment for the rights. The write-off means that CBS overpaid for the rights by about 29 percent. CBS's share price fell by 1.5 percent with the announcement of the write-off. The network has committed to pay over $540 million for the rights to broadcast the next two Winter Olympics, and $1 billion for seven years of college basketball.[14] These contracts also may be a curse.

As an empirical matter, franchise sales at the bottom of the market occur with about twice the frequency of sales at the top of the market. Of the 116 sales in baseball history, 26 were at the top of the market (two or fewer games out of first place), while 51 were at the bottom of the market (thirty or more games out of first place).

Table 5.1   Regression and Maximum-Likelihood Estimates of Sales

Variable	Linear SALE	Logit SALE	Probit SALE
CONSTANT	− .6842	1.2711	.7867
	(9.90)	(3.47)	(3.48)
GAMES BEHIND	− .0330	− .2258	− .1368
	(5.66)	(5.87)	(6.03)
GAMES BEHIND SQUARED	.00072	.00085	.00049
	(6.75)	(6.18)	(6.48)
R^2	.1645	—	—
χ^2	—	59.45	59.08
N	246	246	246

There were 39 sales in between this range. There is no evidence that the timing of the sales is related in any way to the size of the franchise city. Finally, a club with an average reputation will have a lower probability of sale. Average assets exchange at a fair market value; all that a new owner can expect is the average rate of return.

Empirical Evidence of the Timing of Sales

There were 116 sales or partial sales of major league baseball teams between 1901 and 1989.[15] Sales are coded as 1, and the variable is named SALE. The independent variable is GAMES BEHIND; in sale years this value is the number of games behind at the time of the sale. Nonsales are coded 0. The value of games behind for the nonsale years is the average number of games behind over the period. The hypothesized relationship between sales and games behind is quadratic, so the variable GAMES BEHIND SQUARED is included in the estimation. In preliminary estimation interteam effects were considered. None of the team dummies were significant.

The first model estimated is a linear probability model. The results appear in table 5.1 and are easy to interpret. Both GAMES BEHIND and GAMES BEHIND SQUARED are very significant, and the signs are as expected. At a value of zero for games behind, the probability of a sale is .68. At 45.5 games behind the probability of a sale is .68. The minimum probability of a sale is .31 at 22.9 games out of first place. These results seem sensible.

Linear probability models suffer statistical limitations (e.g., predicted probabilities outside of the unit interval, heteroskedasticity). To overcome these difficulties, maximum-likelihood logit and probit models were estimated, and these estimates are also presented in table 5.1.[16] The asymptotic *t*-values are high, with a minimum asymptotic probability of .001 percent. Of course, since the logit model uses the logistic distribution and the probit the cumulative normal distribution function, the coefficient estimates are not readily interpreted. The slope coefficients of the logit and probit can be converted crudely to the corresponding linear probability estimates by multiplying by .25 and .4, respectively.

▼   Profits, Capital Appreciation,
     and the Duration of Ownership
▼

Introduction

Several decades ago sport was more sport than business. The press reported the games, players played for small wages, owners were from the sport and ran the front offices indifferently, and the fans paid a few dollars to see their favorite team beat the visiting club. Nothing in the front office was of any concern except player trades and acquisitions. Now sport is a big business. Many players earn millions of dollars and are celebrities. Some franchises are said to be worth as much as a quarter of a billion dollars (e.g., the New York Yankees, the Los Angeles Dodgers), and at a minimum $30 million. Events like Super Bowl XXVII have entertainers such as Michael Jackson doing the half-time show. Cities fall over themselves to offer sweetheart deals to attract clubs or to keep them from moving. The nexus between economics and sport looms large.

For several decades public policy concerns have been raised about professional sports: Does the restriction on the number of clubs in a league lead to "excess" profits? Do league rules on revenue sharing and exclusivity of franchise territory affect the bottom line sufficiently to preclude small-city clubs from being competitive? Is the fading of family ownership of clubs and the tax-shelter feature of franchises responsible for a more rapid turnover of clubs?

Operating Profits in Sports

As with any business, there are two dimensions to the financial returns of club ownership: annual net cash flow from operations and capital gains from the appreciation of the business. The historical evidence on profitability in team sports is scant. The conventional wisdom is that, except for football, clubs located in small markets are marginal operations that cannot effectively compete with big-city clubs.[1] Given the wide disparity in franchise market size, the view is that big-city clubs earn large monopoly profits, while small-city clubs hang by a thread to survive another day.

Financial World has published estimates of revenues, operating expenses, and net operating income for 102 teams for the 1990 and 1991 seasons, along with estimates of the value of the franchises. These estimates seem to have been made with some care. Their revenue estimates are based on estimates of gate receipts; national, cable, and local broadcasting rights; revenues from luxury boxes; and concession, novelty and licensing fees.[2] Operating expenses were based on estimates of player expenses (salaries, bonuses, insurance, and pensions), promotional expenses, general and administrative costs, and rent and stadium-maintenance costs. A club's operating profit is revenue minus operating expenses.

It is difficult to separate fact from fancy about operational profits in professional team sports for several reasons. As privately owned entities, the clubs have no obligation to reveal their finances. Fearing political scrutiny of their business practices, the teams tend to overstate expenses and understate operating profits in public pronouncements. Stated losses from operations are often a figment of creative accounting. It is not unusual for a club, even one with a losing record located in a small market, to generate a positive cash flow while the books show red ink. This is due in part to the way clubs are purchased. A common method of purchasing a club is for investors to form a separate corporation that owns the club. The investors lend the money for the purchase and receive interest payments. These payments are a cost on the club's books, but are in fact a method of taking a cash flow from its operations. Further, an owner (managing partner) may take a large salary, a generous expense account, insurance, and other benefits. These are operational costs to a club, but may in part represent a profit withdrawal. Moreover, out of the $100 million or so average franchise purchase price, as much as $50 million may be taken as player depreciation (historically depreciated for five years by the straight-line method). As a result a $10 million cost appears on the club's books. These are but a few of the accounting issues in sports that cause skepticism about statements of financial duress in professional team sports.[3]

In my judgment considerable effort was made by *Financial World* to avoid some of these pitfalls in sports-accounting procedures. Nevertheless, one should be somewhat skeptical of their estimates for any particular club. These estimates of club finances are used primarily in determining the average profitability among the sports, and differences in profitability between big-city and small-city clubs, and between winning and losing clubs. Because aggregation tends to cancel out errors in data, conclusions about groups of clubs are on a firmer footing.

The financial estimates for the four sports appear in tables 6.1 through 6.4. The estimates for gross revenue and gross operating profit are the averages for the combined 1990 and 1991 seasons for baseball and football and for the 1989–90 and 1990–91 seasons for basketball and hockey. Averaging the annual observations reduces the season-to-season variance somewhat, thereby offering a more stable picture of the financial aspects of the club and the sport. The win percent is also averaged for the two seasons.

The average baseball club (table 6.1) had revenue of $54.9 million, a standard deviation of $15.7 million, and a range between $37.4 million (Montreal Expos) and $94 million (New York Yankees). Revenues are more unequally divided among clubs in baseball than in football and hockey, but less so than in basketball. As can be calculated from table 6.5 large-city clubs (mean population 8 million) averaged revenues of $61.1 million, compared to $47.7 million for small cities (mean population 2.4 million). The effect of franchise market size and the win percent on revenue is apparent in the regressions in table 6.6. Each 1 million in population in the franchise market yields $2.7 million in revenues. Each .100 point in the win percent (about eight extra games won at home) of a baseball club adds $8.1 million in revenue. Thus an extra home game won is worth about a million dollars in revenue.

Annual club operating profit (return) as a percent of revenue averaged 8.3 percent, with a standard deviation of 12.9 percent, and a

Table 6.1 The Financial Status of Baseball, 1990–1991

Franchise	Revenue (millions)	Profit (millions)	Return (% of revenue)	Value (millions)
Large City, Wins ≥ .500				
New York Mets*	$86.1	$18.3	21.2%	$200.0
Los Angeles Dodgers	71.9	7.5	10.4	200.0
Chicago White Sox*	63.5	13.4	21.1	125.0
Oakland Athletics*	61.4	5.4	8.7	115.8
Detroit Tigers	44.8	1.2	2.6	83.6
Boston Red Sox	75.0	11.5	15.3	180.6
Texas Rangers	55.9	11.5	20.6	100.6
Large City, Wins < .500				
New York Yankees*	94.0	27.5	29.2	225.0
Chicago Cubs*	57.4	7.9	13.7	125.9
Baltimore Orioles†	49.3	10.4	21.0	200.0
San Francisco Giants*	49.5	2.3	4.7	105.0
Philadelphia Phils	55.1	8.0	14.4	130.0
Houston Astros	43.0	0.5	1.2	92.0
Small City, Wins ≥ .500				
Toronto Blue Jays	83.1	20.1	24.2	178.3
Minnesota Twins	42.5	(5.3)	(12.5)	85.7
Pittsburgh Pirates	43.5	(2.4)	(5.4)	82.2
Cincinnati Reds	48.9	5.6	11.5	102.3
Small City, Wins < .500				
Montreal Expos	37.4	1.1	2.9	74.1
Cleveland Indians	38.4	(7.7)	(19.9)	75.0
Atlanta Braves	37.9	3.7	9.6	74.3
St. Louis Cardinals	57.5	11.6	20.2	128.3
Seattle Mariners	39.4	6.0	15.2	71.4
San Diego Padres	47.8	4.1	8.5	99.1
California Angels	51.4	0.6	1.1	102.1
Kansas City Royals	53.4	(8.5)	(15.9)	122.4
Milwaukee Brewers	38.6	(3.8)	(9.7)	80.6

Table 6.1 (*continued*)

Franchise	Gains (annual appreciation)	Years	Total Return	Size (thousands)	Wins
Large City, Wins ≥ .500					
New York Mets*	16.0%	31	37.2%	18,120	.520%
Los Angeles Dodgers	9.9	79	20.3	11,513	.553
Chicago White Sox*	10.6	32	31.7	8,181	.559
Oakland Athletics*	10.5	41	19.2	6,042	.578
Detroit Tigers	17.7	88	20.3	4,620	.504
Boston Red Sox	18.3	79	33.6	4,110	.531
Texas Rangers	12.0	31	32.6	3,766	.519
Large City, Wins < .500					
New York Yankees*	18.0	88	47.2	18,120	.426
Chicago Cubs*	17.7	86	31.4	8,181	.478
Baltimore Orioles†	15.6	89	36.6	6,076**	.443
San Francisco Giants*	16.8	88	21.5	6,042	.494
Philadelphia Phils	16.4	88	30.8	5,963	.478
Houston Astros	13.1	31	14.3	3,641	.432
Small City, Wins ≥ .500					
Toronto Blue Jays	24.1	15	48.3	3,300	.547
Minnesota Twins	17.4	79	4.9	2,388	.522
Pittsburgh Pirates	15.9	90	10.5	2,284	.596
Cincinnati Reds	16.3	89	27.8	1,728	.510
Small City, Wins < .500					
Montreal Expos	9.1	23	12.0	2,900	.483
Cleveland Indians	17.2	75	(2.7)	2,769	.414
Atlanta Braves	17.6	85	27.2	2,737	.491
St. Louis Cardinals	18.8	74	39.0	2,467	.476
Seattle Mariners	16.7	15	31.9	2,421	.494
San Diego Padres	10.5	23	19.0	2,370	.491
California Angels	13.5	31	14.6	2,257	.497
Kansas City Royals	14.6	23	(1.3)	1,575	.486
Milwaukee Brewers	12.5	23	2.8	1,572	.485

Source: Data from *Financial World,* 9 July 1991 and 7 July 1992.

*Designated clubs split the franchise market.

†Since half of the fans attending Baltimore games come from Washington, D.C., that area's population included.

Table 6.2   The Financial Status of Football, 1990–1991

Franchise	Revenue (millions)	Profit (millions)	Return (% of revenue)	Value (millions)
Large City, Wins ≥ .500				
New York Giants	$53.6	$10.3	19.1%	$150.0
Los Angeles Raiders	49.1	8.5	17.2	135.0
Chicago Bears	53.5	11.7	21.9	126.0
San Francisco 49ers	53.6	4.3	7.9	150.0
Philadelphia Eagles	53.9	10.3	19.1	141.1
Detroit Lions	46.4	4.3	9.2	115.7
Dallas Cowboys	54.2	11.6	21.3	180.0
Washington Redskins	48.9	9.1	18.5	125.0
Houston Oilers	51.4	8.1	15.8	119.3
Miami Dolphins	64.2	13.6	21.1	205.0
Large City, Wins < .500				
New York Jets	46.7	6.5	13.8	125.0
Los Angeles Rams	50.5	9.1	18.0	135.0
New England Patriots	42.8	1.5	3.5	99.8
Small City, Wins ≥ .500				
Seattle Seahawks	49.5	5.7	11.5	129.9
Pittsburgh Steelers	46.7	10.1	21.6	112.3
Denver Broncos	47.5	7.6	16.0	113.3
Kansas City Chiefs	47.2	8.3	17.5	122.4
New Orleans Saints	49.1	7.3	14.9	124.0
Buffalo Bills	54.7	10.7	19.6	125.6
Small City, Wins < .500				
Cleveland Browns	55.8	9.3	16.7	145.0
Atlanta Falcons	46.2	4.4	9.5	112.8
Minnesota Vikings	48.2	7.4	15.3	119.1
San Diego Chargers	46.0	4.8	10.3	113.4
Phoenix Cardinals	48.0	8.5	17.7	119.9
Tampa Bay Buccaneers	45.3	4.4	9.6	114.1
Cincinnati Bengals	49.0	5.4	10.9	125.0
Green Bay Packers	43.6	3.8	8.6	115.0*
Indianapolis Colts	46.4	7.2	15.5	116.0

Table 6.2 (*continued*)

Franchise	Gains (annual appreciation)	Years	Total Return	Size (thousands)	Wins
Large City, Wins ≥ .500					
New York Giants	NA	NA	NA	18,120	.657%
Los Angeles Raiders	NA	NA	NA	13,770	.657
Chicago Bears	27.0%	60	48.9%	8,181	.688
San Francisco 49ers	14.4	14	22.3	6,042	.750
Philadelphia Eagles	12.6	42	31.7	5,963	.625
Detroit Lions	11.1	57	20.3	4,620	.563
Dallas Cowboys	NA	NA	NA	3,766	.563
Washington Redskins	15.6	31	34.1	3,734	.750
Houston Oilers	NA	NA	NA	3,641	.626
Miami Dolphins	13.6	26	34.7	3,001	.625
Large City, Wins < .500					
New York Jets	16.1	29	29.9	18,120	.438
Los Angeles Rams	10.7	50	28.7	13,770	.251
New England Patriots	14.6	16	18.1	4,110	.219
Small City, Wins ≥ .500					
Seattle Seahawks	13.1	17	24.6	2,421	.501
Pittsburgh Steelers	NA	NA	NA	2,284	.501
Denver Broncos	15.6	26	31.6	1,858	.532
Kansas City Chiefs	NA	NA	NA	1,575	.657
New Orleans Saints	11.6	25	26.5	1,307	.594
Buffalo Bills	NA	NA	NA	1,176	.813
Small City, Wins < .500					
Cleveland Browns	12.8	38	29.5	2,769	.282
Atlanta Falcons	10.7	26	20.2	2,737	.469
Minnesota Vikings	NA	NA	NA	2,388	.438
San Diego Chargers	10.2	25	20.5	2,370	.313
Phoenix Cardinals	12.4	59	30.1	2,030	.282
Tampa Bay Buccaneers	12.3	17	21.9	1,995	.282
Cincinnati Bengals	14.4	24	25.3	1,728	.376
Green Bay Packers	NA	NA	NA	1,572	.313
Indianapolis Colts	14.2	43	29.7	1,237	.251

Source: Data from *Financial World*, 9 July 1991 and 7 July 1992.

*1992 value of the franchise.

Table 6.3   The Financial Status of Basketball, 1990–1991

Franchise	Revenue (millions)	Profit (millions)	Return (% of revenue)	Value (millions)
Large City, Wins ≥ .500				
Los Angeles Lakers*	$62.4	$30.2	48.3%	$200.0
New York Knicks*	29.7	4.6	15.3	100.0
Chicago Bulls	34.3	12.1	35.3	100.0
Philadelphia 76ers	25.3	3.7	14.7	75.0
Detroit Pistons	46.2	19.4	41.9	150.0
Boston Celtics	36.3	11.5	31.7	180.0
Houston Rockets	25.4	3.0	11.6	58.0
Large City, Wins < .500				
New Jersey Nets*	21.6	1.5	6.9	42.6
Los Angeles Clippers	22.4	2.1	9.2	42.9
Golden State Warriors	25.4	3.3	12.9	50.7
Dallas Mavericks	25.1	3.3	13.1	54.4
Washington Bullets	17.8	(1.9)	(10.4)	37.5
Miami Heat†	24.0	6.4	26.5	58.6
Small City, Wins ≥ .500				
Atlanta Hawks	21.9	0.1	0.2	53.5
Seattle Supersonics	18.1	(2.7)	(14.9)	37.3
Phoenix Suns	25.3	4.5	17.8	99.0
Milwaukee Bucks	21.7	1.6	7.2	53.5
San Antonio Spurs	25.1	4.0	15.7	46.5
Indiana Pacers	19.0	(3.1)	(16.3)	33.3
Portland Trailblazers	28.8	5.9	20.5	59.9
Utah Jazz	21.6	2.1	9.7	44.9
Small City, Wins < .500				
Cleveland Cavaliers	29.0	5.9	20.4	61.1
Minnesota Timberwolves†	25.9	8.7	33.7	51.2
Denver Nuggets	18.6	(2.6)	(13.7)	40.6
Sacramento Kings	22.6	2.7	11.7	49.1
Charlotte Hornets†	28.6	7.9	27.4	59.6
Orlando Magic†	24.9	8.9	35.7	60.8

Table 6.3   (*continued*)

Franchise	Gains (annual appreciation)	Years	Total Return	Size (thousands)	Wins
Large City, Wins ≥ .500					
Los Angeles Lakers*	15.2%	34	63.5%	13,770	.738%
New York Knicks*	NA	NA	NA	18,120	.513
Chicago Bulls	19.2	25	54.5	8,181	.708
Philadelphia 76ers	20.1	28	34.8	5,963	.592
Detroit Pistons	18.7	17	60.6	4,620	.655
Boston Celtics	17.1	40	48.8	4,110	.659
Houston Rockets	15.7	24	27.3	3,641	.567
Large City, Wins < .500					
New Jersey Nets*	18.1	22	25.0	18,120	.262
Los Angeles Clippers	12.4	21	21.6	13,770	.372
Golden State Warriors	NA	NA	NA	6,042	.494
Dallas Mavericks	14.7	11	27.8	3,766	.457
Washington Bullets	14.0	27	3.6	3,744	.372
Miami Heat†	NA	NA	NA	3,001	.257
Small City, Wins ≥ .500					
Atlanta Hawks	12.6	23	12.8	2,737	.512
Seattle Supersonics	13.6	24	(1.3)	2,421	.500
Phoenix Suns	18.5	23	36.3	2,030	.665
Milwaukee Bucks	15.4	23	22.6	1,572	.561
San Antonio Spurs	16.3	15	32.0	1,323	.677
Indiana Pacers	13.8	16	(2.5)	1,237	.506
Portland Trailblazers	14.2	21	34.7	1,188	.744
Utah Jazz	12.4	17	22.1	1,065	.655
Small City, Wins < .500					
Cleveland Cavaliers	14.3	21	26.1	2,769	.457
Minnesota Timberwolves†	NA	NA	NA	2,388	.311
Denver Nuggets	15.3	13	10.2	1,858	.389
Sacramento Kings	NA	NA	NA	1,385	.293
Charlotte Hornets†	NA	NA	NA	1,112	.275
Orlando Magic†	NA	NA	NA	971	.299

Source: Data from *Financial World*, 9 July 1991 and 7 July 1992.

*Designated clubs split the franchise market.

†Recent expansion clubs.

Table 6.4   The Financial Status of Hockey, 1990–1991

Franchise	Revenue (millions)	Profit (millions)	Return (% of revenue)	Value (millions)
Large City, Wins ≥ .500				
Los Angeles Kings	$30.0	$ 6.1	20.3%	$45.0
Chicago Blackhawks	24.3	6.9	28.4	45.0
Boston Bruins	30.4	10.4	34.3	57.4
Large City, Wins < .500				
New York Rangers	27.1	5.4	19.9	54.4
New Jersey Devils	19.7	1.8	8.9	35.0
New York Islanders	26.5	8.6	32.3	51.8
Philadelphia Flyers	22.3	1.7	7.6	42.8
Detroit Red Wings	31.7	11.2	35.3	43.7
Washington Capitals	20.0	0.5	1.3	38.0
Toronto Maple Leafs	23.8	5.2	21.8	45.2
Small City, Wins ≥ .500				
Montreal Canadiens	28.7	6.4	22.1	59.2
St. Louis Blues	19.3	0.8	3.9	31.6
Buffalo Sabres	18.0	2.6	13.3	37.0
Edmonton Oilers	23.7	3.8	15.8	51.6
Calgary Flames	25.1	4.3	17.0	52.0
Small City, Wins < .500				
Minnesota North Stars	16.2	(3.2)	(19.5)	30.0
Pittsburgh Penguins	19.4	2.5	12.9	41.5
Vancouver Canucks	22.6	0.2	0.7	41.6
Hartford Whalers	24.4	3.6	14.8	45.4
Winnipeg Jets	15.5	(1.0)	(6.5)	30.0
Quebec Nordiques	21.5	0.2	0.7	45.0

range from − 19.9 (Cleveland Indians) to 29.2 percent (New York Yankees). The profit from club operations is much larger for the big-city clubs (14.2 percent) than for the small-city clubs (2.3 percent). The regression of market size and win percent on the profit rate appears in table 6.6. Each 1 million in population adds 1.5 percent in profit. While the win percent appears to affect revenue, it has no statistically significant effect on the club profit margin in baseball.

Table 6.4 (*continued*)

Franchise	Gains (annual appreciation)	Years	Total Return	Size (thousands)	Wins
Large City, Wins ≥ .500					
Los Angeles Kings	13.9%	24	34.2%	13,770	.522%
Chicago Blackhawks	24.8	65	53.2	8,181	.582
Boston Bruins	37.1	67	71.4	4,110	.591
Large City, Wins < .500					
New York Rangers	NA	NA	NA	18,120	.491
New Jersey Devils	10.9	17	19.8	18,120	.460
New York Islanders	8.5	19	40.8	18,120	.385
Philadelphia Flyers	13.6	24	21.2	5,963	.429
Detroit Red Wings	24.7	65	60.0	4,620	.432
Washington Capitals	12.2	16	13.5	3,734	.476
Toronto Maple Leafs	11.0	65	32.8	3,300	.394
Small City, Wins ≥ .500					
Montreal Canadiens	25.7	82	47.8	2,900	.535
St. Louis Blues	6.8	24	10.7	2,467	.554
Buffalo Sabres	NA	NA	NA	1,176	.501
Edmonton Oilers	17.4	12	33.2	600	.513
Calgary Flames	NA	NA	NA	600	.597
Small City, Wins < .500					
Minnesota North Stars	11.9	24	(7.6)	2,388	.404
Pittsburgh Penguins	13.5	24	26.4	2,284	.482
Vancouver Canucks	9.7	21	10.4	1,300	.375
Hartford Whalers	16.2	12	31.0	1,068	.460
Winnipeg Jets	12.2	12	5.7	600	.428
Quebec Nordiques	16.1	12	16.8	600	.197

Source: Data from *Financial World*, 9 July 1991 and 7 July 1992.

All clubs in the National Football League make money, even the lowly New England Patriots. A typical club had annual revenue of $49.7 million, with a standard deviation of $4.5 million, and a range from $42.8 million (New England Patriots) to $64.2 million (Miami Dolphins). The high proportion of national broadcast revenue out of total revenue (about 57 percent), evenly split among the clubs, and

Table 6.5   Profit Margins and Total Return by City Size

Category	All Sports	MLB	NFL	NBA	NHL
All Clubs					
Operating margin	$13.2	$ 8.3	$15.1	$15.3	$13.6
Total return	27.0	23.5	27.8	28.1	29.0
Large-City Clubs					
Operating margin	17.6	14.2	15.9	19.8	21.1
Total return	33.3	29.0	29.9	36.8	38.6
Small-City Clubs					
Operating margin	13.2	2.3	14.4	11.1	6.8
Total return	20.5	18.0	26.0	19.3	19.4

Source: Based on data in tables 6.1–6.4.

the more even division of the gate receipts are important factors in reducing the spread in revenues among the clubs. The size of the franchise market has no statistically meaningful effect on club revenue (see table 6.6), but winning does. Each .100 point in the win percent (.8 of a game won at home) is worth an extra $1.24 million in club revenue. Thus an extra game won at home is worth about $1.5 million in extra club revenue.

The operating margin in football is almost twice that in baseball. The average club earned 15.1 percent profit on its revenues, with a standard deviation of 4.9 percent, and a range from 3.5 percent (New England Patriots) to 21.9 percent (Chicago Bears). Again, the size of the franchise market had no statistically significant effect on profits, but increased winning raised profit margins. Each .100 point in the win percent added 1.2 percent in profit (see table 6.6), or 1.5 percent per extra home game won.

While average revenue in basketball is about half of that in football, the operating margin is somewhat larger, and some clubs are extremely profitable. Mean revenue was $26.9 million, with a standard deviation of $9.3 million, and a range from $17.8 million (Washington Bullets) to $62.4 million (Los Angeles Lakers). The inequality in the distribution of revenues in basketball is the highest among the sports. The coefficient of variation in basketball is .35 compared to .29 in baseball. Both the size of the franchise market and the win percent have important effects on revenue. Each 1 mil-

Table 6.6 Regressions Relating Financial Status to Winning and Franchise Market Size, by Sport

Variable	Constant	Win Percent	Population (thousands)	R^2/N
Major League Baseball				
Revenue ($ millions)	0.662	80.675%	.0027	.585
	(0.03)	(1.77)	(5.92)	26
Profit margin (%)	− 16.550	33.768	.0015	.227
	(0.64)	(0.66)	(3.01)	26
Roster cost ($ millions)	− 2.308	43.888	.0004	.184
	(0.22)	(2.10)	(1.88)	26
National Football League				
Revenue	43.222	12.393	.00005	.185
	(17.99)	(2.76)	(0.34)	28
Profit margin	8.716	11.535	.0001	.139
	(3.28)	(2.32)	(0.67)	28
Roster cost	18.783	5.317	.00012	.100
	(11.72)	(1.78)	(1.11)	28
National Basketball Association				
Revenue	9.171	29.378	.0006	.303
	(1.73)	(3.02)	(2.10)	27
Profit margin	.589	24.251	.0005	.002
	(0.05)	(1.15)	(0.81)	27
Roster cost	6.544	6.865	.00013	.474
	(7.55)	(4.33)	(2.67)	27
National Hockey League				
Revenue	11.715	21.522	.00025	.096
	(1.60)	(1.46)	(1.52)	21
Profit margin	− 26.952	76.023	.0008	.159
	(1.27)	(1.78)	(1.73)	21
Roster cost	4.013	6.724	.00002	.048
	(2.03)	(1.68)	(.054)	21

Note: Student t-values are in parentheses.

lion in population raised revenue about $629,000, and each .100 point in the win percent (about four extra home games won) raised it about $2.94 million. An extra game won at home is worth about $720,000.

The average operating margin in the NBA was 15.3 percent, with a large standard deviation (16.9 percent), and a range from −16.3 percent (Indiana Pacers) to 48.3 percent (Los Angeles Lakers). Neither the size of the franchise market nor the win percent have any statistically meaningful effect on profit margins in basketball (see table 6.6).

NHL club revenue averaged $23.5 million, with a standard deviation of $4.6 million, and a range between $15.5 million (Winnipeg Jets) to $31.7 million (Detroit Red Wings). Despite having the smallest amount of media revenue among the sports, a 100–0 gate split, and the widest dispersion in franchise market size (e.g., the Los Angeles Kings play in a market with a population of 13.8 million, while the Calgary Flames, Winnipeg Jets, and Quebec Nordiques play in population centers of around 600,000, revenues in the NHL are less unevenly distributed than in basketball and baseball. This is partly because about half of the clubs have sellout or near sellout seasons (including Quebec, Calgary, and Edmonton). Canadians take their hockey clubs seriously, no matter what. While the win percent and population size have positive effects on revenue ($2.15 million per .100 point in the win percent, and $250,000 per 1 million population) the statistical significance of these estimates is too low to have confidence in them.

As in basketball, the operating margins in hockey vary tremendously. The average profit margin of 13.6 percent is somewhat lower than in basketball and football, but higher than in baseball. The standard deviation in profit margins is 13.9 percent, with a range between −19.5 percent (Minnesota North Stars, who in 1993 left the chill of Minneapolis for the warmth of Dallas) and 35.3 percent (Detroit Red Wings). The range in operating margins in hockey is comparable to that in basketball. Unlike basketball, in which there is no convincing link between franchise market size and winning and profit margins, hockey shows some evidence of a link. Each .100 point in the win percent is associated with about a 7.6-percent increase in the profit margin (about 1.9 percent per extra home game won), and each 1 million in population with about a .8-percent

Table 6.7 Regressions Relating Financial Status to Winning and Franchise
Market Size, All Sports

Variable	Revenue (millions)	Profit Margin	Roster Cost (millions)
Constant	$40.691	−5.087%	$17.336
	(10.41)	(0.93)	(12.89)
NFL	−4.916	7.058	.398
	(2.07)	(2.13)	(0.49)
NBA	−27.671	7.290	−11.007
	(11.56)	(2.18)	(13.38)
NHL	−31.336	6.087	−14.216
	(12.08)	(1.68)	(15.93)
Win Percent	20.418	19.633	7.171
	(2.98)	(2.05)	(3.05)
Population (thousands)	.00076	.0007	.00014
	(4.42)	(2.79)	(2.43)
R^2	.728	.117	.825
N	102	102	102

Note: Student t-values in parentheses.

increase. The statistical significance is only about 90 percent for both coefficients, however, and skepticism is warranted.

Table 6.7 presents a summary of intersport differences in revenues and profit margins and the effect of the win percent and franchise market size on these variables. The variables NFL, NBA, and NHL are categorical variables (equal to 1 for the sport and 0 otherwise), with major league baseball as the reference dummy. In the revenue regression, holding intersport differences constant, each .100 point in the win percent on average is worth $2 million in revenue. Each 1 million in population is worth about $760,000. What is the revenue trade-off rate between the size of the franchise market and the win percent? Average revenue in the sports was $39.7 million, and average population in the franchise market was 5.1 million. A $760,000 revenue gain is about 1.9 percent above average. An increase of 1 million in population above the average franchise market size is a 19.6 percent gain. Therefore the elasticity of revenue with respect to population is 9.8 percent. A .100-point increase in the win percent is 20 percent above the average of .500 and is associated with a 5.1-percent increase in revenue above the average. The elasticity of revenue with respect to the win percent is 25.5 percent. Thus, holding the sport constant, revenue is 2.6 times more sensitive to club performance than to franchise market size. The strong effect of winning on club revenue is a powerful incentive for fielding competitive teams.

Winning in sports means incurring higher operating costs. While it is not axiomatic that plunging headlong into the free-agent market assures a championship, club roster costs and club victories are positively correlated. Table 6.6 contains the regressions relating player roster cost to the club win percent and to franchise market size, and table 6.7 gives the relationship for all of the sports combined. Generally the results relating the roster cost to the win percent are highly significant (the exceptions being football, which is significant at the 91 percent level, and hockey which is significant at the 89 percent level). Because player-initiated movement in football and hockey was restricted, the ability of clubs to bid for prime talent was constrained. As a result, the variance in player roster cost is lower in the NFL and NHL than in baseball or basketball. Moreover the variance in roster cost is higher in baseball than in basketball. The team salary cap (salary floor) tends to reduce the variance in roster cost across clubs somewhat.

The profit-margin regression equation in table 6.7 sheds light on the effect of franchise market size and the win record on the team's bottom line. The NFL, NBA, and NHL are all more profitable than baseball. Holding the sport constant, each 1 million in population adds 0.7 percent to the profit margin. The difference in population size between the average big-city club and the average small-city club is on the order of 6 million, so big-city clubs are 4–5 percent more profitable than small-city clubs. The elasticity of the profit margin with respect to the franchise market size is .034. Each .100 point in'the win percent adds about 2 percent to the profit margin. The average spread between the most successful club and the least successful across the sports is about .400 in the win percent, which translates into an 8-percentage-point difference in the profit rate. The elasticity of the profit margin with respect to the win percent is .098. Thus the effect of winning on the club's bottom line is 2.9 times that of franchise market size and is comparable to the effect on team revenue. Winning in team sports not only generates revenue for a club but greatly affects the profit margin. Is it any wonder that baseball and basketball owners bid aggressively for star-caliber free agents?

Capital Appreciation of Sports Franchises

Generally, the profit margin in professional team sports is quite good, and for some clubs it is extraordinary. What of capital gains? Casual empiricism suggests that the value of a typical franchise rises over time. Historically, owners have been able to count on substantial capital gains at the time of sale. For example, despite the lower price forced on Bob Lurie by other owners, the sale of the San Francisco Giants to the San Francisco investors netted him $95 million. The Lurie interests had paid $10 million for the club in 1977. The Houston Astros sold for $17.9 million in 1979 and $95 million in 1992. Eli Jacobs bought the Baltimore Orioles in 1988 for $70 million and sold the club in 1993 for $174 million. Multi-million-dollar gains in the value of sports franchises have been the rule in all sports in recent times.

What has been the historical rate of appreciation of sport franchises? Are there differences in capital appreciation rates by sport? Are the appreciation rates skewed among clubs based on franchise market size? These are the questions examined here. The data utilize the *Financial World* estimates of the 1991 values of professional team franchises (tables 6.1–6.4) and earlier information on prior sales contained in Quirk and Fort.[4] I was able to extract information on prior sales for eighty-three clubs. *Financial World*'s 1991 values of the franchises are determined by multiplying gross revenue by a factor of 2 and adjusting the result for other important considerations (e.g., the valuation of the team's stadium if privately held, favorable lease arrangements). These are estimates, however, not exchange prices. As such, the estimated values of particular franchises, like the estimated profits, should be treated skeptically. In particular the estimates of the value of basketball franchises seem somewhat low. NBA broadcast revenue has about doubled since the late 1980s, and player salary share has been stabilized. For example, the 1992 value of the San Antonio Spurs was estimated at $63 million. In February, 1993, B. J. (Red) McCombs agreed to sell the club to a group of local investors for $75 million. The struggling Dallas Mavericks were said to be worth $60 million. The Mavericks were for sale in 1992 with an asking price of $95 million. There have been no takers at this price. As in the analysis of operating profit, however, the emphasis here is on differences among the sports.[5]

The mean franchise value of the eighty-three clubs in 1991 was $94.5 million, with a standard deviation of $50 million and a range from $30 to $225 million. A football franchise is marginally more valuable than a baseball franchise ($129.4 versus $121.5), with a lower variance ($23.9 versus $46.4). The lower variance in football franchise values naturally follows from a lower variance in revenues. A typical basketball franchise is worth $71.4 million, with a standard deviation of $46.8 million, while an average hockey franchise is worth $43.9 million, with a standard deviation of $8.6 million. Average franchise values clearly differ among the sports, although the difference between football and baseball is not statistically significant.

While inspection of tables 6.1–6.4 reveals that franchise values are correlated with franchise market size, we might ask if the rate of capital appreciation is related to the type of sport or to the franchise market size. Owning a sport franchise is more risky than owning treasury bonds, but the risks across sports should be the same. Efficient capital-market theory would suggest that no significant differences should exist in returns by sport or by size of the market. This is a testable hypothesis.

Tables 6.1–6.4 give the 1991 value, the years between the earliest known exchange price and the 1991 estimated value, and the internal rate of return for eighty-three franchises. The mean annual capital appreciation (under Gains) is 15.1 percent, with a standard deviation of 4.5 percent. The mean financial appreciation rates by sport were 15.3 percent in baseball, with a standard deviation of 3.5 percent; 15.6 percent in basketball, with a standard deviation of 2.3 percent; 13.7 percent in football, with a standard deviation of 3.6 percent; and 15.9 percent in hockey, with a standard deviation of 7.6 percent. Tests for significance of the differences in the means reveal no significant effect by sport. Moreover, capital appreciation rates were regressed on metropolitan population of the franchise, number of teams in the metropolitan area, and population divided by number of teams in the area. The simple correlations were, respectively, .0051, .0571, and .0064. It is fair to conclude that there are no differences in the rates of return by sport or by market size.

Total Return to Franchise Ownership

The total return to franchise ownership is annual profit plus capital gain. The capital appreciation rates were added to the profit margins and appear in tables 1 through 4 (under Total Return). For all sports the total return during the early 1990s was 27 percent per year. Big-city clubs had higher total returns than small-city clubs (33.3 percent versus 20.5 percent). The range in total returns is quite large. Table 6.8 ranks the most- and the least-profitable clubs. The

Table 6.8   Most-Profitable and Least-Profitable Clubs in the Early 1990s

Club	Total Annual Return
Most Profitable	
Boston Bruins, NHL	71.4%
Los Angeles Lakers, NBA	63.5
Detroit Pistons, NBA	60.6
Detroit Red Wings, NHL	60.0
Chicago Bulls, NBA	54.5
Chicago Blackhawks, NHL	53.2
Chicago Bears, NFL	48.9
Boston Celtics, NBA	48.8
Toronto Blue Jays, MLB	48.3
Montreal Canadiens, NHL	47.8
New York Yankees, MLB	47.2
Least Profitable	
Minnesota North Stars, NHL	−7.6
Cleveland Indians, MLB	−2.7
Indiana Pacers, NBA	−2.5
Seattle Supersonics, NBA	−1.3
Kansas City Royals, MLB	−1.3
Milwaukee Brewers, MLB	2.8
Washington Bullets, NBA	3.6
Minnesota Twins, MLB	4.9
Winnipeg Jets, NHL	5.7

Source: Data from *Financial World*, 9 July 1991 and 7 July 1992.

Boston Bruins are estimated to be earning an annual return of 71.4 percent. Big-city clubs such as the Bruins, the Red Wings, and the Blackhawks are extraordinarily profitable in hockey, while the Lakers, Pistons, Bulls, and Celtics do very well in basketball. The club losing the most during the early 1990s was the Minnesota North Stars, a club playing in a moderate-size city and with not too poor a record on the ice. The club subsequently moved to Dallas. Other clubs that lost money (negative total return) were the Cleveland Indians (the financial bleeding should stop when they move into their new stadium), Indiana Pacers, Seattle Supersonics, and Kansas City Royals. Generally, the clubs hanging by a financial thread are in small cities.

Can we conclude that monopoly profit exists in professional sports? An annual rate of return of 27 percent for an average club is very attractive. The median profit as a percent of sales (revenue) for the 500 largest industrial corporations typically ranged from 3.9 to 5.5 percent over the period 1975–89.[6] Investors in the stock market obtain gains in stock prices and dividends of about 10 percent per year. Thus, compared to profits in large corporations or the risky alternative of the stock market, the return to franchise ownership is much larger.

Two important antitrust cases attacked the monopoly of Standard Oil and U.S. Steel. Both firms had very large shares of the domestic market. Jones estimated the rate of return of Standard Oil over the period 1882–1906 at 19.8 percent and of U.S. Steel (over the period 1901–1910) at 12.1 percent.[7] However, the rate of return to a sample of large manufacturing firms from 1915 to 1929 was 17 percent.[8] Oil is a risky business, and therefore Standard Oil's return does not seem out of line. Compared to restricted competition in the oil or the steel business, the return in team sports still seems high. On the other hand, when I visited Hong Kong, a very competitive economy, a few years ago, I observed a commercial real estate boom in progress. Since a Communist Chinese takeover is scheduled for 1997 I was perplexed at the level of commercial real estate (a nonmoveable resource) investment activity. In discussions with Hong Kong businessmen I learned that three years was the normal investment recovery period, an implicit rate of return of 26 percent. If such a return in a very competitive capitalist economy is a normal rate of return, then the average return to ownership of sports franchises should not be judged as excessive.

If we consider profit relative to revenue in a market where the government restricts entry, as in commercial television, the return to sports-franchise ownership is lower. Affiliated television stations across all markets had profits as a percent of revenue of 21.8–29.9 percent over the period 1975–89.[9] As with sports franchises, this is only one component of the total return to a television license. During the 1980s TV stations typically sold at prices between ten to twelve times cash flow, and large capital gains were earned at the time of sale.[10] Using net revenue data for the average affiliated station over the period 1975–89, I calculated that the average annual nominal appreciation rate of a television station license was 11.6 percent.[11] Added to the average profit percentage of 26.6 percent, this yields a total return of 38.2 percent per year. This total return percentage is higher than for sports franchises, but it is biased downward for purposes of comparison. Affiliated television stations operate in large and small broadcast markets, while most clubs operate in large markets. Network affiliates operating in the top ten markets in 1989 had average profits of 38 percent of revenue.[12] Assuming no difference in the growth rate of revenue between large- and small-market stations, which seems reasonable, the total return to license ownership for these stations was about 50 percent per year in the late 1980s. As with sports franchises, the profitability of affiliated stations is correlated with market size. Stations located in the small markets (below the top 100 in size) reported aggregate accounting losses.[13] As in sports accounting, however, losses may not reflect economic losses.

While I will leave it to the reader to judge whether the return to ownership in professional sports contains a monopoly component, I think it would be fair to conclude that a number of clubs do evidence a monopoly return. If a 30-percent or greater return to franchise ownership is taken as evidence of monopoly, then about half of the clubs in professional team sports earn a monopoly return.

The Duration of Ownership

For how long are clubs held before they are sold to other investors? Are there differences in the tenure of ownership among the sports? I was able to construct a sample of 387 franchise sales in the history of the four team sports.[14] A histogram of ownership tenure for the 387 cases is given in figure 6.1. Mean tenure of ownership is 10.9 years, the standard deviation of tenure is 11.7 years, and the range

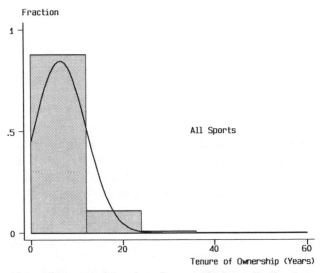

Figure 6.1   Histogram of duration of ownership for professional sports clubs.

is from 1 to 68 years. Histograms of ownership tenure by sport are given in figure 6.2. While the distributions in all of the sports are skewed, there are apparent differences among them. Football has the longest average tenure of ownership at 13.2 years, with a standard deviation of 14.3 years, and a range of from 1 to 68 years. Baseball has a mean tenure of 11.2 years, with a standard deviation of 11.9 years, and a range of from 1 to 66 years. Hockey has a mean tenure of 11.8 years, with a standard deviation of 12.3 years, and a range of from 1 to 65 years. Tenure of ownership is shortest in basketball, with a mean of 7.6 years, and a standard deviation of 6.5 years (the range is from 1 to 42 years). As will be discussed below, there is some weak statistical support for the proposition that ownership tenure is somewhat longer in football and somewhat less in basketball.

The change in type of ownership from family to corporate or syndicate ownership and the rise of sports as a tax shelter have been identified as sources of a greater turnover of franchises.[15] The conventional wisdom is that the new corporate and syndicate investors in sports are more concerned with financial return than with bringing a championship to the home-town fans.

During the early 1950s Bill Veeck reasoned that player contracts ought to be expensed at the time of the purchase of a franchise. The IRS partially bought into the scheme. It agreed to the straight-line depreciation of player contracts over their useful lives. Since player contracts are a substantial portion of the franchise assets, a wonderful tax shelter was born. From 1951 to 1963 the top marginal tax rate was 91–92 percent. Top tax rates were still around 75 percent during the 1960s and 1970s. In a number of instances 90–100 percent of the franchise purchase price was allocated to player contracts during this period. In a number of leagues, clubs were incorporated as Subchapter S corporations, which permitted book losses from team operations to be used to shelter income from other (nonteam) sources. The tax-shelter aspects of franchise ownership were thought to induce a more rapid turnover of franchises. Teams were sold as the depreciation allowance was exhausted. Significant tax-shelter aspects of sports franchise ownership existed for twenty-five years (1950–75). In the mid-1970s [*Laird v. United States,* 391 F. Supp. 655 (N.D. Ga. 1975)], the IRS clamped down on the amount of the franchise purchase price that could be allocated to player contracts (basically 50 percent or less). With this change, and with lower top marginal tax rates, the tax-shelter aspects of franchise ownership have been greatly eroded and have impinged on post-tax cash flow. Furthermore, besides limiting the amount of the franchise that can be allocated to player contracts, the Internal Revenue Service has been fairly tough in limiting other tax-shelter aspects of franchise ownership. While other franchise owners can amortize the "goodwill" of the business, sports teams cannot. Moreover, broadcast rights [*Laird; McCarthy v. United States,* 807 F. 2d (1986)], exclusive territorial rights, and parking and concessions are considered part of the franchise value and are not depreciable. As the value of the broadcast rights rises, the depreciable component of the franchise price at the time of sale declines. In basketball and baseball, player contracts as the depreciable fraction of the sale price have fallen to the 33–40-percent range. The end of player reservation has shortened the period of depreciation. With unlimited free agency, the value of player contracts to a club would be zero. Even less of the sale price may be depreciated in football.

We have suggested that there is some support for the view that during the tax-shelter period (1950–75), turnover of franchises might have been accelerated. The mean duration of ownership dur-

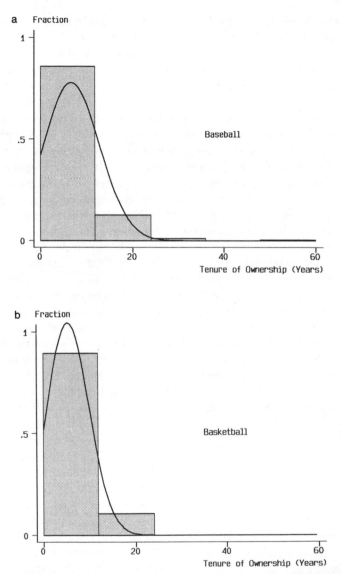

Figure 6.2   Histograms of duration of ownership for baseball, basketball, and football clubs.

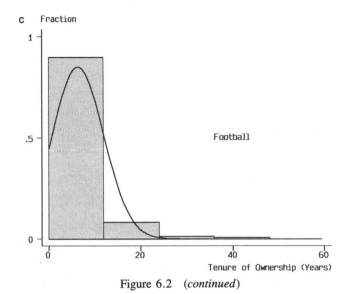

Figure 6.2 (*continued*)

ing the period of the tax shelter was 11.7 years, with a standard deviation of 10.1 years; during the periods prior to and after the tax shelter, it was 10.5 years, with a standard deviation of 12.5 years. The difference in the means is not statistically significant.

To test statistically the relationship between duration of ownership and the effects of the more liberal tax-shelter environment during 1950–75, survival analysis was employed. Specifically a maximum-likelihood, proportional-hazard model was estimated, with three sport dummies (football, basketball, and hockey) and a tax-shelter dummy as the covariates. As expected, the hockey and tax-shelter dummies were not significant. The model was reestimated with just the basketball and football dummies as regressors.[16]

The coefficient of the football dummy on the hazard rate was − .2252. Thus the hazard rate is lower, and hence the survival probability is higher in football. The coefficient is weakly statistically significant.[17] The coefficient of the basketball dummy on the hazard rate was .2480. Thus the hazard rate (survival probability) is higher (lower) in basketball. The coefficient is statistically stronger than in football, but is still rather weak.[18] While it is true that the survival probability in football is higher and in basketball it is lower, the differences with baseball and hockey are neither dramatic in a statistical sense nor large.

△

△

△ **PART FOUR**

▼ The Market for Coaching Talent

▼

▼

▼ Managerial Performance and Tenure

▼

Introduction

There has been a great deal of theorizing about the role of management in organizations but little testing of hypotheses. The reasons are obvious. Private firms have no incentive to reveal data about their operations unless legally required to do so. Measures of corporate performance such as stock prices vary for reasons other than the quality of the management team. Public entities (e.g., bureaucracies, the military) produce outputs that are ambiguously measured. Moreover, many organizations are extremely complex, which makes the linking of managerial decision making with a metric of the firm's performance difficult. The bulk of the empirical research has been in the sociology of organizations. The main issue in this literature is whether leadership matters at all, or whether institutional constraints restrict the ability of individuals to act. Organizational sociologists tend to believe in a rather extreme form of structuralism: The institutional constraint set matters, not the individual manager.

Many observers of sports believe that managers and coaches are important to a club's performance. Frequent changes in field leadership are made in the search for improved team performance—managers in baseball and head coaches in basketball only last about three years. Very few (about 10 percent) survive ten or more years (see table 7.1). While tenure is longer in football (on average, 4.2 years) it is probably less than that of managers in other lines of business. Is this high turnover of field management a useless strategy, or is it a valid attempt to improve club performance?

Table 7.1   Frequency Distribution of Managers and Head
Coaches by Years of Experience

Years	Baseball	Basketball	Football
<1	23.1	22.7	9.1
1	27.0	26.2	19.0
2	11.1	17.4	16.3
3	7.6	9.2	10.4
4	5.7	5.3	10.0
5	4.6	2.1	5.4
6	4.3	1.8	7.2
7	2.8	3.2	5.0
8	2.0	2.5	2.3
9	1.5	2.1	3.2
10	1.5	0.7	2.3
11–14	3.7	3.5	4.1
15–20	3.5	3.2	3.2
21 +	1.7	0.0	2.7
N	541	282	221

For economists the main problem in the theory of organizations is the alignment of managerial objectives with that of the owners (shareholders). Shareholders have a simple objective function that they wish maximized: the wealth of the firm. Managers may have different goals. For example, they may wish to control a larger amount of resources within the firm, perceiving that size of staff supervised is correlated with pay and promotion. To maximize the wealth of the firm, however, resources within it need to be allocated across employments so that no redistribution of resources will increase output (i.e., the theory of the firm as a miniature capital market). This conflict of goals between managers (agents) and owners (principals) is known as the principal/agent problem.

In sports the analogy is the owner(s)/manager or owner(s)/head-coach problem. When acquiring information and monitoring performance is costly, managerial shirking, malfeasance, and incompetence may exist. Such agent deficiencies reduce the residual to the principal. In team sports a reduced effort by the manager or head coach yields fewer games won than would be possible if the playing

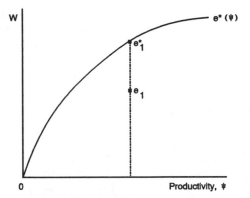

Figure 7.1 Coaching efficiency (effort): The relationship between club win percent and player productivity.

talent available were directed with maximum effort and competence. The relationship between a club's win percent and its profit is well known.[1]

Consider a simple production process, as in team sports. Let output (wins), W, be produced with a random productivity parameter, ψ, that captures some multidimensional measure of team playing talent, and coaching or manager effort, e. Higher player productivity, ψ, and/or greater coaching effort, e, yield increased levels of the manager's expected performance. In the usual treatment of the problem, the principal (owner) and the agent (head coach or manager), who are both risk-neutral, have similar information about the random productivity parameter, but the owner cannot observe the realization of ψ or the level of managerial effort. Figure 7.1 illustrates the deterministic case: $W = e\psi$. The owner desires that for all realizations of ψ, the coach should expend the efficient level of effort, $e^*(\psi)$. The line segment $e^*(\psi)$ may be viewed as the efficiency or production frontier. When the coach shirks or is incompetent and expends effort e_1, as in the figure, the principal loses a residual per unit equal to e_1/e_1^*. The ratio e/e^*, which is in the unit interval, is a measure of managerial effort or efficiency.[2]

Of course this characterization of the principal/agent problem is static. It is the case of one owner dealing with one agent in a vacuum. In the more dynamic setting that characterizes team sports, the level of managerial effort or efficiency should increase over time. Sports is known as a very data-intensive business; information is widespread and cheap. Owners and managers know the latest performance statistics on the players. Even in a vacuum, over time an owner will learn by experience and should be able to distinguish good from bad field management. Through hiring and firing, the level of managerial quality should tend to increase over the owner's tenure.

Team sports are produced interactively. A game is a joint product of two firms (teams). Teams compete with each other in leagues, playing more or less the same set of competitors on a regularly scheduled basis. Reliable and cheap information is available about all clubs in the league. Each owner can observe the effort or efficiency of his field manager or head coach compared to the field management of the other clubs. Competition between clubs and cheap information about performance tend to drive out managerial incompetence and slack. Competition ought to yield positive selection of field management similar to positive selection of playing talent. If so, over time competition will tend to raise the average level of managerial effort and reduce its dispersion, which is a testable hypothesis. This argument also implies that competent managers and head coaches will tend to survive longer and that those who are incompetent or who are shirking will be fired more frequently. The length of managerial tenure in professional team sports ought to be linked to coaching quality.

Measuring Coaching Quality

Winning means outscoring the opponent. Scoring (runs in baseball, points in basketball and football) is determined by offensive skills relative to the opponent's defensive skills: $s = f(X_i)$, where X is the ith offensive skill relative to its defensive counterpart. Opponent scoring is the result of defensive skills relative to the opponent's offensive skills: $os = g(Y_i)$, where Y is the ith defensive skill relative to its offensive counterpart.

In baseball, hitting is the main offensive skill, but once a player has reached base, he may be advanced (steal, hit-and-run, pinch hit, etc.). Bases advanced are correlated with runs scored. Pitching and fielding are the main defensive skills. Clubs devote considerable scouting resources to determining their opponents' hitting weaknesses (e.g., types or positions of pitches and the portion of field that hits are likely to occur). In basketball, shooting percentages (field goal and free throw), offensive rebounds, assists, and turnovers are the main measures of offensive skill. Blocked shots, steals, defensive rebounds, and fouls are the main measures of defensive skills. Generally, coaching inputs are higher in basketball and football than in baseball. Clubs develop certain playing strategies (e.g., fast break or a more deliberate pace of play, set offensive plays and defensive strategies) that do not work equally well against all opponents. Particularly toward the end of a close game, head coaches make nearly continuous playing adjustments and play calls. In football the main measures of offensive skills are offensive blocking, quarterback pass-completion rates and yards per pass, receiver completions and yards per pass, running back yards per carry, and kicker three-point field goals and conversions. Defensive skills are measured mainly by defensive blocking, tackles, quarterback sacks, interceptions, fumble recoveries, and so on. Football teams also develop certain offensive and defensive styles of play. When the set strategies are not working, the ability to adjust offense and defense at halftime partly measures head-coaching ability.

Let us define the total regular season scoring (S) and opponent scoring (OS) as follows: $s = \Sigma\, s = \Sigma\, f(X_i)$, and $OS = \Sigma\, os = \Sigma\, g(Y_i)$. Then the club win percent for the regular season, W, is functionally related to scoring relative to opponent scoring.

$$
\begin{aligned}
W &= F(S/OS) \\
&= F\left[\frac{\Sigma f(X_i)}{\Sigma g(Y_i)}\right].
\end{aligned}
\tag{7.1}
$$

For statistical estimation, the form of the model is

$$
\ln W = \beta_0 + \beta_1 \ln(S/OS) + \varepsilon.
\tag{7.2}
$$

There are certain attractive statistical properties in this formulation: W is bound between 0 and 1, and because one team's victory is by definition another club's loss, the win percent has a constant mean (.5). Because there are a large number of contests over a season and through time, the theoretical variance is constant across time subsamples. By definition, runs or points scored during a regular season must equal opponent runs scored. Obviously S/OS has a constant mean of 1 (a mean of 0 if the specification is $S - OS$). Of course scoring has not been constant in professional sports due to rule changes and innovation (e.g., movement of the pitcher's mound to 60' 6", the introduction of the lively ball, the banning of a spitball and scuffball in baseball; the forward pass and the field goal in football; the jump shot, the three-point shot, and the twenty-four-second clock in basketball). Any change that increases scoring, however, also increases opponent scoring. Specifying the independent variable in relative rather than absolute form yields a constant variance. It is expected that the error term will be normally distributed with constant variance across time.[3] Hence, under this formulation, it is possible to measure managerial efficiency through time within a sport and to compare it across sports.

The job of field management is to win as many games as possible with the playing talent at hand. This is achieved by maximizing scoring, minimizing opponent scoring, and transforming that relative scoring production into wins. Scoring (S) is maximized when all offensive skills relative to the opponents' defensive skills are equated at the margin.[4] Opponent scoring (OS) is minimized when all defensive skills relative to the opponents' offensive skills are equated at the margin.[5] Such aspects of managerial quality are allocative in nature. Given the playing talent at hand, scoring is maximized and opponent scoring is minimized by allocating offensive and defensive skills in such a manner that not one extra run or point can be produced or an opponent's one extra run or point avoided by a redistribution of playing assignments at any moment of time. Much of the estimating of managerial or coaching quality has been done in this spirit. The empirical analysis utilizing this approach may suffer from an omitted-variables bias; that is, some important independent dimension of playing skill may be omitted (e.g., hustle, aggressiveness, anticipation, clutch performance). Ascribing the difference between potential and actual wins to the coaching function may be inappropriate. In baseball the number of measured dimensions of playing skill is the greatest, and in football the least. Moreover, while the assumption of a linear homogeneous production function is reasonable in baseball, it is less reasonable in basketball, and probably not valid in football (football involves more team production, there are more important interactions among player inputs).

I will assume that managers and coaches allocate their offensive and defensive playing skills in such a way as to maximize scoring and minimize opponent scoring; I take it that the observed S and OS are S_{max} and OS_{min}. The aspect of managerial quality that is measured here is the actual win percent relative to the potential win percent, given S and OS. The measure of coaching quality is $0 < W/W^* \leq 1$, where $W^* = \hat{W} + \varepsilon_{max}$.

The potential win percent (W^*) is obtained from the predicted win percent ($\hat{W}$) plus the largest observed positive residual (ε_{max}), utilizing equation (7.2). The greatest positive error is associated with that manager or head coach who achieved the largest actual win percent compared to the predicted win percent with the observed ratio of scoring to opponent scoring. The efficiency of this best-practice field manager is unity. All other head coaches or managers will lie in the unit interval.[6]

Empirical Results

Data were collected on the win percent, points or runs scored during the season, and opponent points or runs scored from standard sports record sources.[7] The estimated win functions for the three team sports appear in the appendix to this chapter in 7A.1 (see appendix, at end of this chapter). The ratio of team runs (points) scored to opponent runs (points) scored is associated with a high proportion of the variance of the win percent in baseball and basketball (89 and 73 percent, respectively), but with less in football (58 percent). This pattern in the adjusted coefficient of determination across the sports is not surprising. The theoretical standard deviation is inversely proportional to the square root of the sample size. Hence the variance within a season of football (16 games) is much larger than in baseball (162 games). The standard deviations of the win percent for the sports were .096 (baseball), .15 (basketball), and .216 (football). The corresponding standard deviations of relative runs or points were .208, .059, and .463. Baseball has the lowest variance in the win percent and a moderate amount of variance in the ratio of runs scored to opponent runs scored. While basketball has a larger variance in the win percent than baseball, it has a much lower variance in the ratio of scoring to opponent scoring (obviously, this explains the larger coefficient than in baseball in the table). Football has much higher variance both in the win percent and in relative scoring. The coefficient estimates in the table indicate about a unit elasticity of relative run production on winning in baseball, a somewhat more elastic response in football, and a very elastic response in basketball. Raising the relative point production in basketball from 1.0 to 1.01 raises the win percent from .500 to .525.[8]

Players as Managers: Divided Responsibility and Loyalty

It was common for players to serve as managers in the early history of baseball and basketball, but less so in football. This practice gradually faded, although Pete Rose was playing and managing at Cincinnati in 1985 and 1986, and Dave Cowens did the same for the Boston Celtics in the 1978–79 season. Over the history of baseball (1876–1989), 15.3 percent of those who managed a season were player-managers. Historically in basketball (1938–1990), about 9.5 percent were both players and head coaches. In the early years of football, there were some player-coaches (e.g., George Halas), but none in the period studied here.

There is a problem of divided responsibilities and loyalties for a player who also is field manager or head coach. In 1985 Pete Rose was trying to catch Ty Cobb's all-time record of 4,197 career hits. At 44 years of age, "Charlie Hustle" was well past his prime. He appeared in 119 games that from the team's point of view might have been better served by a younger talent. More generally, a player-manager probably cannot do both jobs equally well. Even if he acts exclusively in the owner's interest, he is part of the roster. As a player, his loyalties are likely to be divided. He seeks to do the owner's bidding but continues to seek the respect of his teammates. Comradeship and hard decisions that produce victories but spare no player's feeling are incompatible.

A test of the hypothesis of lower efficiency among player-managers appears in table 7A.2 in the appendix. The dummy variable is equal to one for player-managers in the sample. The coefficient is a measure of the difference in the mean efficiency ratings of the two groups. On average, there is a one-point lower efficiency for player-managers in baseball. Player–head coaches in basketball are less efficient by about five points. In both sports the efficiency differences are statistically significant at above the 99 percent level. The difference in the size of these efficiency effects between the sports may be an indication of the greater demands of the coaching function in basketball than in baseball.

Competition and Dynamic Improvements in Efficiency

Does coaching quality improve over time, as I have theorized? To test for this phenomenon, means and standard deviations of efficiency were calculated for each year in each of the sports and regressed against trend and trend squared. The results appear in table 7A.3 in the appendix. Average coaching efficiency rises over time, and the deviation in coaching quality falls in all sports. The pattern is quadratic in baseball and basketball. The peak in average efficiency in baseball and the minimum in its variance occurred about a decade ago. In basketball it occurred in the late 1960s to early 1970s. Except for the mean level of efficiency in baseball, serial correlation was absent. The regression that appears in the table is corrected for serial correlation. In football there is a linear trend in average efficiency and its variance.

All of the coefficients appearing in the table are highly statistically significant. Examination of the coefficients reveals differences in the rate of improvement in coaching quality among the sports. The average level of managerial efficiency is highest in baseball, but the rate of improvement in the average quality of field managing is lowest. For a period of time, say fifty years, the increase in the average level of managerial efficiency in baseball was from .754 to .775, or about 2.1 points. The reduction in the dispersion of coaching quality was about 4.1 points, or from .101 to .06. In basketball and football the increase in the mean level of head-coaching efficiency is larger: 6.0 and 6.7 points, respectively. The reduction in the standard deviation of coaching quality was 3 points for basketball and 5.2 points for football.

Longevity and Coaching Effort

Perhaps the professional team-sports industry is unique in the sense that all firms have near-perfect knowledge not only of their own production function and player inputs but of their competitors'. One result of this information-rich environment and of interclub competition is that managerial effort or competence is measurable. If compe-

Table 7.2   Veteran Managers and Head Coaches Ranked by
Efficiency

Baseball	Basketball	Football
Frank Selle	Red Auerbach	John Madden
Al Lopez	Larry Brown	George Allen
Billy Martin	Joe Lapchick	Bum Phillips
Earl Weaver	Doug Moe	Buddy Parker
Walt Alston	Don Nelson	Don Shula
Sparky Anderson	Al Cervi	Chuck Knox
Billy Southworth	Lenny Wilkens	Vince Lombardi
Joe McCarthy	Jack Ramsay	Bud Grant
Charlie Comiskey	Al Attles	Sid Gillman
Clark Griffith	Red Holzman	George Halas

tition reveals incompetence and managerial slack, inept coaches should have short careers, and superb managers should have longer careers. The efficiency indicators that were constructed from the residuals from equation (7.2) and that attempt to capture coaching quality should be correlated with length of tenure.

I calculated means and standard deviations of efficiency for all of the managers with two or more career seasons. The top ten with a decade or more of experience are ranked for each of the sports in table 7.2. Table 7A.4 in the appendix presents the regressions of the logarithm of career efficiency and the standard deviation of career efficiency on the logarithm of the length of the managing or coaching career. Previous research has revealed a managerial learning curve: Efficiency rises at a decreasing rate over career length.[9] To capture this phenomenon of learning by doing, the standard deviation of efficiency is included as a regressor.

All of the coefficients are highly statistically significant. The geometric means of the variables for each of the sports were as follows: for baseball, years = 5.0, mean efficiency = .7716, and standard deviation of efficiency = .0396; for basketball, 4.1, .7071, and .088; and for football, 4.9, .561, and .125. What level of improvement in effort or efficiency does it take for a manager or coach to survive one year more than the mean tenure? The predicted required improvement in efficiency in baseball is 3 points (i.e., from .772 to

.802). The predicted required improvement in basketball is 7.7 points (i.e., from .707 to .784). The required improvement in football is 12 points (i.e., from .561 to .681). The required improvement in football seems rather high, but the mean efficiency of head coaches with five or less years of experience was .518 compared to .626 for those with six or more years. The difference in mean efficiency between these two groups is statistically significant.[10] There appears to be a strong screening at around the fifth year of head coaching. If the coach is superior, he stays in professional football; if not, he heads for the college circuit. As some support for this conjecture, the mean efficiency of coaches with six and seven years experience was compared with the mean of coaches with eight or more years. No statistically significant difference was found.[11]

Conclusions

There is more to career longevity than managerial efficiency. No matter how good a manager is at squeezing performance from his players, if the club always finishes in the cellar, the manager will be fired. This is done partly to assure the fans and sports writers that something credible is being done to improve the club. Naturally, managers and head coaches who survive the longest in the leagues tend to have higher win records. The correlation between managerial efficiency and club win percent is known.[12] Nevertheless, a winning record is not completely necessary to managerial survival. Managers or head coaches who have directed a roster of second-rate players have endured. Casey Stengel managed a fine roster when he was with the Yankees, but his record was poor with Boston and the Mets. His lifetime record was .508. Lou Boudreau, Jimmy Dykes, Bucky Harris, Rogers Hornsby, Connie Mack, Gene Mauch, John McNamara, Bill Rigney, Chuck Tanner, and others managed more than a decade or so (Connie Mack endured for fifty-three years) with records well under .500. In football Bart Starr coached Green Bay to a 52–76 record from 1975–83, John McKay at Tampa Bay had a 44–88 record over the period 1976–84, and Webb Ewbank could not achieve a .500 record with the New York Jets from 1963 to 1973.

Managerial efficiency improves over time in all of the sports. The view that competition drives out incompetence and makes it more detectible is not shared by students of the sociology of organizations. Organizational sociologists seem to think that managerial superiority requires great strategic power in the market in which the organization transacts. They believe that competition so restricts the degrees of managerial freedom that one does not observe differences among competitive firms along any dimension. Hence they conclude that management does not matter in a competitive environment. That is simply not true. Talented managers make their competitive firms prosper. Incompetent managers lead their firms into bankruptcy. In sports, bankruptcy is losing. Competition and shared knowledge of the production function sort out the good from the bad managers.

Appendix to Chapter 7

Table 7A.1   Win Production Functions in Team Sports

Sport	Constant	Coefficient	$R^2/(N)$
Baseball			
ln W	$-.7145$	$.9649$ ln (R/OR)	.8880
	(453.18)	(125.44)	(1985)
Basketball			
ln W	$-.7476$	5.0332 ln $(PTS/OPTS)$	.7266
	(117.87)	(47.70)	(857)
Football			
ln W	$-.8410$	1.3513 ln $(PTS/OPTS)$	.5845
	(56.36)	(38.61)	(1060)

Table 7A.2   Managerial Efficiency for Player-Managers Versus Managers

Sport	Constant	Coefficient	$R^2/(N)$
Baseball			
Efficiency	.7763	$-.9915E-02$	.0028
	(514.44)	(2.57)	(1985)
Basketball			
Efficiency	.7368	$-.5133E-01$	.0118
	(156.35)	(3.35)	(857)

Table 7A.3 Changes in Coaching Quality over Time

Sport	Constant	Trend	Trend^2	R^2/DW
Baseball, 1876–1989				
Mean	.7538	.5431E − 03	− .2590E − 05	.5651
Efficiency	(240.47)	(4.39)	(2.51)	2.25
Standard	.1010	− .1111E − 02	.5879E − 05	.4639
Deviation	(21.46)	(5.88)	(3.69)	1.87
Basketball 1938–1990				
Mean	.6737	.4275E − 02	− .6135E − 04	.4337
Efficiency	(71.59)	(5.32)	(4.25)	1.64
Standard	.1637	− .3045E − 02	.5080E − 04	.0637
Deviation	(10.67)	(2.32)	(2.16)	1.54
Football, 1933–1989				
Mean	.5503	.1336E − 02		.3653
Efficiency	(71.22)	(5.76)		1.65
Standard	.2043	− .1041E − 02		.2323
Deviation	(24.92)	(4.24)		1.60

Table 7A.4 Managerial Tenure and Managerial Efficiency

Sport	Constant	ln *EFF*	ln *SD EFF*	R^2/(N)
Baseball				
ln *YEARS*	3.8321	4.7176	.3080	.1382
	(11.29)	(4.90)	(5.48)	(267)
Basketball				
ln *YEARS*	2.6662	2.1354	.2145	.1631
	(9.26)	(5.30)	(2.41)	(142)
Football				
ln *YEARS*	2.6186	.9616	.2308	.1389
	(10.85)	(4.88)	(2.54)	(156)

▼ Does Firing the Manager Improve
Club Performance?

▼

Introduction

As indicated in the previous chapter, economists believe that individuals matter a great deal in organizations, even if the marginal impact
of management cannot be measured very well. Senior management
in complex organizations is attained after long years in jobs of lower
responsibility where performance and judgment are monitored. Promotion through various levels of responsibility is usually based on
merit. Organizations that advance personnel on merit have superior
survival probabilities.

While considerable resources are devoted to *ex ante* screening at
the time of hiring or promotion, mistakes are made in the selection
of managers. Where there is an imperfect match between the principal and the agent, there is one of two outcomes: termination and
replacement, or retention of the manager with possible harm to the
firm. Tracing the effect of managerial performance at the margin on
the firm's prosperity is difficult, not only because business organizations are complex, measures of the output(s) and inputs of the firm
ambiguous, and comparative data on other firms in the same line of
business difficult to obtain, but generally the long history of each
firm as its prospects ebb and flow with successive changes in management is unknown. Only in sports do we find data at the firm
level in such detail.

There is a wide array of data in professional team sports on output
(games, win percent), inputs (player performance), ownership, and

managers. The data record for baseball is very long, and for some teams it is reasonably long for basketball and football. The firms within a sport are identical in many respects, in that they produce identical outputs, use the same units of input skills, compete under the same set of rules, employ the same production function, share a common technology, and so on. They differ in the size of their franchise markets and have different managers and owners at different moments in time.

I have shown that managerial turnover is rather high in sports: about three years in baseball and basketball. Is this churning of managers and coaches rational? Generally, a change in the manager or head coach is justified on the basis of improving the club's revenues through an improvement in the team's record. If the club improves under new field management, the decision to fire the previous coach was rational. Here I model the decision to terminate or retain the manager and test its effect on club output (the team's standing) for baseball and basketball. The empirical analysis is confined to baseball and basketball because they have the largest number of games over a season and hence the least random variance in the output measure.

A Theory of Managerial Termination

The fans of some losing clubs are loyal and tolerant for a while, but mostly fans are fickle: they stay away unless the team is credible on the playing field. I can illustrate the relationship between a club's change in performance and its change in attendance. Figure 8.1 plots the change in each major league baseball club's attendance and the club's change in its win percent between the 1990 and 1991 seasons. While there is considerable variance around the regression line, the relationship is statistically significant at the .004 percent level. Each extra game won at home (an increase in the win record of 1.23 points) raised the average club's attendance by 3,478. At an average ticket price of about $10.00, an extra game won at home is worth about $43,000 in gross gate receipts.

A club is profitable or not depending on its drawing power. Fans obviously have a greater demand for victories than defeats. The club's record over a season depends on the quality of its players relative to those of other clubs in the league, on the management of

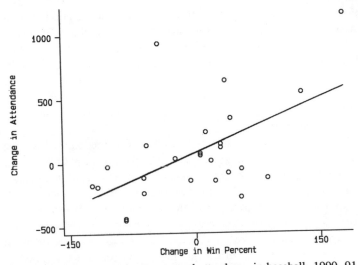

Figure 8.1 Change in win percent and attendance in baseball, 1990–91.

that playing talent as an effective, competitive force on the playing field, and on luck.

Teams allocate considerable resources to identifying and developing playing talent. On occasion a gifted athlete will appear who performs at the level of his endowed gift, but many apparently superior athletes fail to perform well enough to make a major league roster. A long list of Heisman trophy winners, first-round draft choices, and promising minor leaguers is testimony that raw athletic talent and college or minor league performance are only the necessary conditions for success in the professional leagues.

Given a certain level of athletic ability and seeding in the minor or amateur leagues, a rookie's prospects are improved by coaching and by competing in the big leagues. One important function of the field manager and his coaching staff in baseball or the head coach and his assistants in the other sports is to develop talent and to motivate the players. Not all managers and coaches are equally good at this task. Dick Williams succeeded Billy Herman as manager of the Boston Red Sox for the 1967 season. Herman had led the team to a 62–100 record in 1965 and a 64–82 record before he was terminated toward the end of the 1966 season. Williams inherited virtually the same player roster for the 1967 season. The changes that Williams made in the regular roster were the substitution of rookie Reggie Smith at center field for the aging Don Demeter, the replacement of George Smith at second base with Mike Andrews, and the acquisition of aging pitcher Gary Bell from Cleveland. Reggie Smith developed later into a quality player with a .287 lifetime batting average over a seventeen-year career, but in 1967 he batted only .246. What had occurred was that the team had gotten better: a .255 team batting average for the 1967 season versus a .240 average in 1966 and a 3.36 ERA versus a 3.92 ERA. Carl Yastrzemski and Jim Lomborg had the best performance of their careers: Yastrzemski hit .326 with forty-four homers, compared to his .278 batting average and sixteen home runs in 1966, and Lomborg won twenty-two games, twelve more than his 1966 record. While Boston had languished in the cellar in the 1965 and 1966 seasons (forty and twenty-six games respectively out of first place), the club won the pennant in 1967.

Such turnarounds cannot always be ascribed to coaching. Consider the Boston Celtics. Under Tom Heinsohn, Boston was in first place during the 1971–72 to 1975–76 seasons. The club began a slide in playing performance in 1976–77, and collapsed in 1977–78 and 1978–79 by finishing twenty-three and twenty-five games behind the leader. Replacing the head coach did not affect the club's performance. Then Bill Fitch was hired for the 1979–80 season, and the club finished in first place. But was Fitch or Larry Bird responsible for the club's turnaround? When Buffalo's owner John V. Brown swapped franchises with Celtics' owner Irv Levin, Red Auerbach would not surrender Boston's draft pick, the eligible junior Larry Bird. Bird played his senior year at Indiana State, came to the Celtics, started, and won Rookie of the Year. Then the Celtics acquired Robert Parrish and Kevin McHale to replace the retiring Dave Cowens and eventually the aging Nate Archibald. Fitch was elected Coach of the Year. But with the club nine games behind after the 1982–83 season, he was fired unceremoniously. His replacement, K. C. Jones, led essentially the same team to first-place finishes from the 1983–84 to the 1987–88 seasons. This suggests that it was the playing talent more than the coach that turned the Boston Celtics around beginning in the 1979–80 season.

Beyond identifying and developing playing talent, a manager or head coach allocates playing talent during a game (season) and chooses a set of plays or makes playing decisions in a way that maximizes the win percent of the club. This means allocating player time optimally and selecting plays that have a better-than-even chance of succeeding. Additionally, players have a strong incentive to maximize their individual performance statistics, because performance and pay are highly correlated. A manager or head coach must constrain this tendency, because it is team effort that maximizes the probability of a club victory.

Luck plays a role in winning. Statistically, luck is measurable. For normally distributed events (games), the distribution is bell-shaped. Two-thirds of the events lie within one standard deviation of the average. By definition, the average win percentage in team sports is .500. The theoretical standard deviation is related to the number of games, g, played over a season. As indicated previously, among a group of clubs of equal playing strength, the theoretical standard deviation over a season is equal to $.500/\sqrt{g}$. Because of the large number of games in baseball, the theoretical standard deviation is relatively small. In basketball the theoretical standard deviation is larger, and in football it is the largest (about three times that of baseball). Truly superior and inferior clubs are readily identifiable, but some of the year-to-year fluctuation in team standings in baseball and quite a lot of that fluctuation in football can be attributed to random factors that are beyond the control of the players or managers and head coaches. Hence the effect of managerial change in football is not treated here.

We formalize the discussion by defining the win (production or output) function, W (win percent at time t), as the transformation, M, by the field manager or the head coach, of a vector of team playing skills relative to league playing skills, T^i, and luck, or white noise, ϵ.

$$W_t = M_t(T_t^i) + \epsilon_t = W_t^* + \epsilon_t. \tag{8.1}$$

Each variable, the transformation function, and the error term are time-subscripted. Managers and head coaches learn by doing. A manager with a number of years of experience is likely to be better at transforming playing talent into victories than a rookie manager.

Equation (8.1) is a simple formalization of the principal/agent problem. As in the previous chapter, we assume that both the club owner and the manager are risk-neutral and have symmetrical knowledge about player quality, T^i. However, the club owner cannot observe the realization of that player quality, W^*, or the white noise, ϵ. Alternatively, W^* may be viewed as the deterministic part of the managerial or coaching function, and ϵ is the stochastic part.

The owner wishes to maximize profit. This is done by maximizing the win percent (revenue) subject to the level of playing talent fielded (this cost largely is set at the beginning of the season). When all elements of playing talent are allocated so that they are equal at the margin, the win percent is maximized. Hence, with the time subscripts suppressed,

$$\sum_i (\partial W/\partial T^i) T^i = W_{max} + \epsilon. \tag{8.2}$$

Poor managerial performance (incompetence, malfeasance, or shirking) is measurable. It is measured as W^*/W_{max}, which is in the unit interval. The owner observes the win percent, W, but there is a divergence between the actual and the potential win percent because of a lack of managerial effort, $W^* < W_{max}$, and because of luck, ϵ. The decision to retain or fire a manager or head coach based on the observed win percent or standing of the club during or at the end of the season, then, is likely to be subject to error.

In the empirical analysis that follows, the retention/termination decision is based on only one performance measure, the club's standing or rank relative to other clubs in the league. The club's standing is the most important metric that influences the retention/termination decision. For both owner and manager, it is the bottom line. However it is an imperfect measure of managerial effort for the reasons given above. At the time the determination of the manager's status is made by club ownership, other factors known to them but not observed by outsiders are utilized. These may include comparative judgments about player quality and win records among competitors, the personality (e.g., Billy Martin was characterized as contentious; Tommy Lasorda is characterized as easygoing) or management style of the coach, the attitudes of the players toward the coach (especially the superstar players), owner-manager friendship or antagonisms, and so on. Past reputation and experience of the manager may delay termination when the club's record is poor. In addition, some owners think they know a great deal about the game. Their proximity to and knowledge of the game may affect the quality of their judgment on firing or retaining the manager. One cannot discount the possibility that the owner(s) wants to signal quality change to the fans without actually improving club quality (the Texas Rangers' firing of Billy Valentine may be a recent example), or that the owner wants to stir up the pot (e.g., consider a quality team such as the Buffalo Bills that perennially winds up in second place).

Empirical Evidence Regarding Managerial Termination

The Decision to Terminate

In the empirical results that follow, the decision to terminate or retain the manager or head coach is related to the standing (rank) of the club during or at the end of the season. Baseball managers are fired during the season with some frequency, but this happens less often in basketball. The difference between the sports is due to the greater role of coach-specific playing style, strategy, and play-making in basketball. The dependent variable is binary: it is equal to 1 if fired; equal to 0 if retained for the following season. Most managerial change is involuntary, but some coaches and managers do voluntarily change teams or retire, and some die during their tenure. None of the voluntary changes are taken into account here. I treat all changes as involuntary, and this weakens the empirical relationship to some degree. Moreover, the range of club standings is not time-invariant. Before baseball had division play, a club standing was from 1 to 8 (10 with expansions in 1961 and 1962). With division play, in 1969 the worst finish was 6th (7th with the later expansion in the American League). The range is wider in basketball (from 4 to 7) and depends on the number of teams in the league. If terminations are cardinally related to club standing, this difference in the range of club standings through time will weaken the empirical findings. However, if terminations are ordinally related to club standing (e.g., first- or second-place managers are retained with a high probability, while all other finishes lead to a high chance of termination), then these differences in the range of club finishes do not matter very much. As a cross-check to the rank of the club, the win percent was used in the empirical estimation. The win percent is a less desirable measure with regard to the manager's status, because there is wide variation in the record that yields first (second, etc.) place. Although it is rare, some clubs have won their divisions with records as high as .800 or so and as low as .500 or so. Some clubs have been in the cellar with records of .500 as well as records of .250. Statistically, the win percent yielded somewhat inferior results than the rank of the club.

The simplest model estimated is a linear probability model. Its advantage is that the coefficient estimates are easily interpreted. However, such models suffer some disadvantages: the error term is not normally distributed, the predicted probabilities can lie outside of the unit interval, and the coefficient estimates can be biased and inconsistent. It is conventional to estimate maximum-likelihood logit and probit models at least as a cross-check on the linear probability model. The logit model uses the logistic distribution, and the probit model uses the cumulative normal distribution function; thus, the coefficient estimates are not readily interpreted. The logit and probit slope coefficients can be converted crudely to the corresponding linear probability estimates by multiplying by .25 and .4, respectively. The maximum-likelihood estimators of these models are asymptotically normal with all of the desirable properties. Asymptotic *t*-values appear under the coefficient estimates in the logit and probit models in the tables that follow. In addition to the log likelihood, a coefficient of determination is presented for the logit and probit models. The R^2 is obtained by regressing the observed on the fitted proportions. This makes for ease of comparison with the linear probability model.

Baseball   The estimated probabilities of being fired depending on the club's standing appear in table 8A.1 in the appendix to this chapter. The results are for each of the original National and American league franchises. The data are from 1901 to 1989. Where managers were terminated during the season, the record at that time was utilized in the empirical analysis. The club's record during the remainder of the season was not considered. There are eighty-nine observations for each club.[1]

All of the coefficient estimates are positive, and all are highly statistically significant, except those for the Los Angeles Dodgers, the Saint Louis Cardinals, and the logit and probit estimates for the Oakland Athletics, all of which are significant at above the 5 percent level. The range in the coefficient estimates in the linear probability model for the National League is from .033 (the Dodgers) to .098 (for Cincinnati), and in the American League the range is from .038 (the Oakland A's) to .113 (the Detroit Tigers). The average propensity to fire for each one-rank increase in the club standing is .066 percent in the National League and .077 percent in the American League. For an average club with a rank of about 4, the chance of a manager being fired is about 27 percent in the National League and 29 percent in the American.

Basketball For basketball the data are for the original and surviving NBA clubs. The period of coverage is from 1949–50 to 1989–90 ($n = 41$). The probability estimates for basketball appear in table 8A.2 in the appendix. The fact that there are approximately half as many games in a season of basketball as in baseball brings the expected weakening of the statistical estimates. The probability coefficients for the New York Knicks, the Celtics, and the Sacramento Kings are highly statistically significant (at the 1-percent level or above), those of the Atlanta Hawks and the Lakers are significant at 5 percent or above, those of the Golden State Warriors at somewhat above the 5 percent level, and those of the Detroit Pistons are not significant at a reasonable level.

The average probability of being terminated for each one-rank increase in club standing is .112 percent, with a range from .056 percent (for Detroit, with the coefficient being statistically insignificant) to .168 percent for the Kings, but this range in the coefficient estimates overstates the probability of being fired. A standing of third in the division is about a .500 finish. The average probability of being terminated is 31 percent, with a range from 25 percent at Sacramento to 36 percent at Atlanta.

Is Managerial Termination Rational?

I judge it rational to terminate the manager or the head coach only if there is a reasonable expectation that new field leadership will improve the standing of the club. If we observe that club records improve, these terminations are rational; if the records do not improve, then managerial change is irrelevant.

To answer this question, I make a very simple specification. I regress the change in the club's standing between the following year and the current year (i.e., a one-period lead) on the status of the manager in period *t*. The specification is a pretty strong test of the proposition, and it is biased toward not finding a relationship. New coaches inherit a great deal from their predecessors, including many of the starting players. Generally, not many changes in player personnel occur in the first season under a new manager or head coach. A new coach needs some time to become familiar enough with player skills to use them effectively. In addition, it is not necessarily true that the new manager or head coach is much better than the old. When considering managerial change, owners search across the available set of managers. The best of them are probably already employed. Therefore, when a change in field management is considered, the search process may not be successful. For example, the Chicago Cubs fired Frank Chance after a second-place finish (win percent .607) in 1912. A string of managers led the team to successively lower finishes: Johnny Evers (1913), Hank O'Day (1914), Roger Bresnahan (1915), and Joe Tinker (1916). After the fifth-place showing, Fred Mitchell took over the helm. The club turned around for the 1918 season. In more modern times there was a long string of managers at Finley's Oakland A's from 1975 to 1980: Al Dark, Chuck Tanner, Jack McKeon, Bobby Winkles, Jim Marshall, and the mercurial Billy Martin. In basketball there has been a long and unsuccessful search by the Sacramento Kings for a winning head coach since the 1983–84 season: Cotton Fitzsimmons, Jack McKinney, Phil Johnson, Jerry Reynolds, Bill Russell, and Dick Motta.

It would not be appropriate to consider leads longer than one season or to ignore unsuccessful managerial changes (i.e., cases where the managers or head coaches that succeeded a terminated manager were also fired). As time passes, there is more that is different about the club that is being managed. Player turnover in a club is considerable, with average player careers in the range of five to seven years in baseball and basketball. By constraining ourselves to a one-year change in the club's standing, we are assured that most of the change can be attributed to the manager or head coach.

The empirical estimates for baseball are presented in table 8A.3 and for basketball in table 8A.4 in the appendix to this chapter. There are eighty-eight observations for baseball and forty for basketball. The expectation *a priori* is that managerial change is rational, meaning that the sign of the regression coefficient is negative. For baseball all of the coefficients are negative, six of them are statistically significant at the 1-percent level or above, four at the 5-percent level, four at the 10-percent level, and two are not significant. For the National League the average of the coefficients is $-.99$, and for the American League it is -1.07. As a result, it is safe to conclude that, on average, a new manager raises the standing of a baseball club by one rank.

For the reason given above, the evidence from basketball is weaker. The signs are mainly (six of the seven cases) correct, but the coefficients for the Atlanta Hawks, Boston Celtics, and Detroit Pistons are not statistically different from zero. The largest coefficient is that of the Golden State Warriors. There, a change in the head coach is associated with an improvement of two ranks in the standing of the club. But taking all of the clubs into account, the average improvement in standing is about two-thirds of a rank.

Does Ownership Matter?

Connie Mack, "Mr. Baseball," was a marginal ball player (1886–96) but managed for an exceptionally long time (1894–96 at Pittsburgh; 1901–50 at Philadelphia). He was part owner of the Philadelphia A's. Until 1913, majority control of the club was with baseball manufacturer Benjamin Shibe. Connie Mack bought out Frank Hough and Sam Jones, who had a 25-percent share in the club. He became an equal partner with Shibe. Mack took care of the club on the playing field, and Shibe watched the finances. The Mack family sold their interests in the club in 1954 to Arnold Johnson, who moved the team to Kansas City. Mack died shortly thereafter.

Many older fans and sportswriters believe that one of the things wrong with baseball today is that there are no more owners like Connie Mack. It is said that the owners of today don't have baseball in their blood. Increasingly, the owners are businessmen who have succeeded elsewhere, in brewing or broadcasting, or something else, who own the clubs as the fun part of a portfolio of holdings. It is believed that the game would be better if there were more owners with traits like those of Bill or Phil Wrigley, Charlie Ebbets, Walter and Peter O'Malley, Barney Dreyfus, John Galbreath, Bob and

Rudy Carpenter, Charles and Horace Stoneham, Tom Yawkey, Charles and Lou Comiskey, and Clark and Calvin Griffith. They bought clubs, often as a sole source of income, and frequently passed them on to their children. Some blame baseball entrepreneur Bill Veeck, who not only put a midget at bat, 3'6" Eddie Gaedel, and originated the exploding scoreboard, but invented club ownership as a tax shelter. Others blame television for the tremendous rise in broadcast revenues that has escalated franchise prices to the stratosphere. The $100 million or so for a baseball franchise makes single ownership of a club as a family business unlikely. Now clubs are purchased by syndicates of investors, one of whom serves as the managing partner.

The assertion of the benefits of family ownership implies that there are tangible differences between these clubs and those held more as a business investment. There is a belief (I will show that it is a myth) that owners like Tom Yawkey and some others would spend whatever was necessary to win on the playing field and that, being close to the day-to-day operations of the team, they would somehow make decisions more in the interest of producing a winning record.

First, we examine whether long-term ownership improves decisions about terminating or retaining the manager. In table 8A.5 the linear probability model is reestimated with the addition of ownership slope dummies (i.e., owner times finish). The slope dummy should capture any difference in the propensity of long-term owners to fire the manager relative to other owners of the club at other times. I can see no *a priori* reason to believe that long-term owners are any better at this aspect of decision making than other owners. Hence the appropriate significance test is two-tail.

By my criterion there were twenty-seven long-term owners. Connie Mack does not appear because he was also the manager. In the case of the O'Malleys, except for Chuck Dressen (1951–53), only Walt Alston (1954–76) and Tommy Lasorda (1977–) have managed the club. There were only four highly significant coefficients of the twenty-seven owner dummies: Phil Wrigley (a probability of .077 percent versus .149 percent for the club under other ownership), Clark Griffith (.044 versus .083), George Steinbrenner (.19 versus .056), and Charles Finley (.086 versus .009). Apparently Wrigley and Griffith were relatively tolerant of managerial failure, but Steinbrenner and Finley were brutal. Interesting as this might be, the few significant cases preclude a conclusion that long-term ownership has any effect whatever on the managerial termination/retention decision.

We might expect long-term owners to be better at picking successful replacement managers, but this is not the case. Only five coefficients are significant at about the 10 percent level in table 8A.6. The coefficient that stands out is that of Charles Stoneham: a −5.7 change in the rank after firing the manager. The result is an anomaly. In 1919 a syndicate that included Stoneham acquired the Giants from the heirs of John T. Brush. John McGraw had been manager since 1903. He continued as manager until 1932, when his health declined, and he was replaced after forty games by Bill Terry. In 1932 the club finished eighth in the standings, but won the pennant in 1933 under Terry. Thus Stoneham, who died in 1936, had only two managers for the club.

Despite the lack of evidence that long-term owners are any better at managerial change, perhaps they are more committed to winning. To test this proposition, the season record of the long-term owners was compared with the season record of other club owners. A *t*-test on the means was conducted. For the National League it was an even bet: seven of the long-term owners had better and seven had worse records than the other owners of the team. Few (five of fourteen) differences were statistically significant. Similar results were found for the American League. Despite the myth, it appears that who owns a club does not matter very much for the fan.

Conclusions

The function of a manager or head coach is to maximize the residual claim of the owner(s) by maximizing the club win record with the available set of player inputs. A bottom-division finish is evidence of poor-quality players or poor field management. In general the two can be distinguished.

Here the decision to retain or terminate the field management was modeled and estimated. Owners use the club's standing as a major source of information about managerial quality. For an average club, each one-place drop in its standing increases the probability that the manager will be fired by about 7 percent in baseball and about 11 percent in basketball.

Changing the field management is only the necessary condition for improving the club's standing. The replacement must be better for termination to be preferred to retention. It appears that managerial termination is rational in sports: in baseball the club's record improves one rank in the team standings; in basketball the average improvement is about two-thirds of a rank in standing.

Finally, it is a myth that ownership matters. There is a belief that only long-term ownership by people with the sport in their blood induces them to part with their money and field the kind of quality team that will bring a championship. Moreover, people think that it takes time and hands-on control of the club for an owner to learn to make decisions that are in the best interest of the club. There is no empirical evidence to support this myth. Long-term owners are no better than other owners at making judgments about managerial quality or at fielding clubs with better records.

Appendix to Chapter 8

Table 8A.1 Probability Estimates of Managerial Termination in Baseball

	Linear: Fired	Logit: Fired	Probit: Fired
National League			
Atlanta Braves			
Constant	.559E − 02	− 2.380	− 1.453
	(0.04)	(3.12)	(3.30)
Finish	.713E − 01	.348	.212
	(2.85)	(2.64)	(2.75)
R^2	.075	.115	.110
Log likelihood	—	− 54.60	− 54.56
Chicago Cubs			
Constant	.232E − 01	− 2.232	− 1.376
	(0.21)	(3.71)	(3.92)
Finish	.793E − 01	.373	.229
	(3.57)	(3.17)	(3.33)
R^2	.128	.201	.193
Log likelihood	—	− 52.78	− 52.69

Table 8A.1 (*Continued*)

	Linear: Fired	Logit: Fired	Probit: Fired
Cincinnati Reds			
Constant	$-.855E-01$	-3.052	-1.825
	(0.84)	(4.34)	(4.71)
Finish	$.978E-01$	.507	.304
	(4.74)	(3.92)	(4.15)
R^2	.205	.265	.261
Log likelihood	—	-47.66	-47.62
Los Angeles Dodgers			
Constant	$.152E-01$	-3.340	-1.699
	(0.22)	(4.01)	(4.58)
Finish	$.327E-01$	.284	.147
	(2.01)	(1.91)	(1.90)
R^2	.044	.011	.013
Log likelihood	—	-33.24	-33.31
Philadelphia Phils			
Constant	.155	-2.315	-1.415
	(0.12)	(3.34)	(3.53)
Finish	$.676E-01$	.325	.199
	(3.09)	(2.85)	(2.96)
R^2	.099	.114	.110
Log likelihood	—	-53.99	-53.94
Pittsburgh Pirates			
Constant	$.492E-02$	-2.600	-1.529
	(0.05)	(4.15)	(4.47)
Finish	$.587E-01$	.330	.191
	(2.92)	(2.70)	(2.73)
R^2	.089	.013	.010
Log likelihood	—	-44.68	-44.71
St. Louis Cardinals			
Constant	$.934E-01$	-1.948	-1.175
	(0.98)	(3.54)	(3.75)
Finish	$.469E-01$	.237	.142
	(2.24)	(2.16)	(2.19)
R^2	.055	.010	.010
Log likelihood	—	-50.40	-50.39

Table 8A.1 (*Continued*)

	Linear: Fired	Logit: Fired	Probit: Fired
San Francisco Giants			
Constant	$-.331E-01$	-3.013	-1.820
	(0.42)	(4.57)	(4.96)
Finish	.702	.433	.263
	(3.30)	(2.91)	(3.05)
R^2	.111	.001	.001
Log likelihood	—	-38.74	-38.46
American League			
Baltimore Orioles			
Constant	$-.536E-01$	-2.984	-1.761
	(0.49)	(3.92)	(4.27)
Finish	.755	.417	.246
	(3.76)	(3.29)	(3.45)
R^2	.140	.113	.106
Maximum likelihood	—	-48.63	-48.63
Boston Red Sox			
Constant	$.656E-01$	-1.992	-1.219
	(0.64)	(3.67)	(3.83)
Finish	$.640E-01$	.294	.181
	(3.14)	(2.90)	(2.96)
R^2	.102	.192	.189
Log likelihood	—	-52.93	-52.91
Chicago White Sox			
Constant	$-.145$	-3.488	-2.070
	(1.30)	(4.33)	(4.68)
Finish	.102	.560	.334
	(4.51)	(3.75)	(3.92)
R^2	.189	.251	.245
Log likelihood	—	-46.33	-46.33
Cleveland Indians			
Constant	$-.298E-01$	-2.507	-1.525
	(0.22)	(3.43)	(3.61)
Finish	$.898E-01$	.427	.260
	(3.23)	(2.95)	(3.06)
R^2	.107	.188	.183
Log likelihood	—	-53.65	-53.64

Table 8A.1 (*Continued*)

	Linear: Fired	Logit: Fired	Probit: Fired
Detroit Tigers			
Constant	−1.79	−4.335	−2.563
	(1.91)	(4.58)	(5.02)
Finish	.113	.740	.439
	(5.35)	(4.00)	(4.27)
R^2	.248	.205	.199
Log likelihood	—	−39.58	−39.35
Minnesota Twins			
Constant	.137	−2.369	−1.442
	(0.11)	(3.43)	(3.63)
Finish	.650E−01	.323	.197
	(2.94)	(2.73)	(2.82)
R^2	.090	.057	.057
Log likelihood	—	−52.62	−52.57
New York Yankees			
Constant	.806E−01	−1.979	−1.205
	(1.03)	(4.30)	(4.56)
Finish	.702E−01	.335	.204
	(3.34)	(2.97)	(3.05)
R^2	.113	.123	.120
Log likelihood	—	−48.88	−48.83
Oakland Athletics			
Constant	.697E−01	−2.201	−1.294
	(0.77)	(3.69)	(4.00)
Finish	.380E−01	.213	.122
	(2.40)	(2.28)	(2.31)
R^2	.062	.007	.005
Log likelihood	—	−48.00	−48.05

Table 8A.2   Probability Estimates of Managerial Termination in Basketball

	Linear: Fired	Logit: Fired	Probit: Fired
Atlanta Hawks			
Constant	.949E − 01	− 1.814	− 1.107
	(0.61)	(2.35)	(2.44)
Finish	.887E − 01	.399	.243
	(1.81)	(1.73)	(1.76)
R^2	.078	.137	.134
Log likelihood	—	24.73	− 24.74
Boston Celtics			
Constant	− .865E − 01	− 3.375	− 1.971
	(0.93)	(3.67)	(4.13)
Finish	.135	.791	.458
	(3.37)	(2.47)	(2.65)
R^2	.226	.098	.083
Log likelihood	—	− 14.95	− 14.88
Detroit Pistons			
Constant	.163	− 1.470	− .923
	(0.94)	(1.81)	(1.86)
Finish	.558E − 01	.248	.157
	(1.13)	(1.13)	(1.15)
R^2	.032	.021	.022
Log likelihood	—	− 25.67	− 25.65
Golden State Warriors			
Constant	.608E − 01	− 2.080	− 1.291
	(0.35)	(2.22)	(2.32)
Finish	.735E − 01	.359	.224
	(1.62)	(1.57)	(1.62)
R^2	.063	.018	.018
Log likelihood	—	− 24.27	− 24.23
Los Angeles Lakers			
Constant	− .105E − 02	− 2.611	− 1.582
	(0.09)	(3.19)	(3.44)
Finish	.115	.626	.381
	(2.03)	(1.84)	(1.92)
R^2	.095	.002	.002
Log likelihood	—	− 18.52	− 18.42

Table 8A.2 (Continued)

	Linear: Fired	Logit: Fired	Probit: Fired
New York Knicks			
Constant	−.136	−3.473	−1.982
	(0.72)	(2.62)	(2.88)
Finish	.141	.788	.445
	(2.57)	(2.24)	(2.37)
R^2	.145	.137	.122
Log likelihood	—	−22.34	−22.43
Sacramento Kings			
Constant	−.253	−4.307	−2.615
	(1.53)	(3.17)	(3.44)
Finish	.168	.964	.585
	(3.92)	(2.92)	(3.15)
R^2	.282	.361	.355
Log likelihood	—	−19.87	−19.72

Table 8A.3 Improvement in Club Standing and Managerial Termination
          in Baseball

Club	Constant	Fired	R^2
National League			
Atlanta	.232	−.638	.027
	(0.94)	(1.55)	
Chicago	.364E−01	−.309	.008
	(0.16)	(0.83)	
Cincinnati	.345	−1.145	.075
	(1.37)	(2.65)	
Los Angeles	.132	−1.132	.027
	(0.49)	(1.56)	
Philadelphia	.304	−.710	.030
	(1.15)	(1.63)	
Pittsburgh	.418	−1.608	.112
	(1.75)	(3.30)	
St. Louis	.317	−1.157	.041
	(0.99)	(1.92)	
San Francisco	.169	−1.228	.049
	(0.66)	(2.10)	

Table 8A.3   (*Continued*)

Club	Constant	Fired	R^2
American League			
Baltimore	.183	− .790	.030
	(0.67)	(1.63)	
Boston	.439	− 1.213	.067
	(1.51)	(2.48)	
Chicago	.525	− 1.488	.105
	(2.02)	(3.17)	
Cleveland	.214	− .621	.024
	(0.84)	(1.46)	
Detroit	.446	− 1.533	.095
	(1.71)	(3.01)	
Minnesota	.525	− 1.629	.092
	(1.66)	(2.96)	
New York	.206	− .686	.023
	(0.80)	(1.41)	
Oakland	.123	− .601	.016
	(0.47)	(1.18)	

Table 8A.4   Improvement in Club Standing and Managerial Termination
in Basketball

Club	Constant	Fired	R^2
Atlanta Hawks	.185	− .339	.012
	(0.66)	(0.68)	
Boston Celtics	− .303E − 01	− .398	.013
	(0.13)	(0.70)	
Detroit Pistons	− .192	.407	.029
	(0.85)	(1.07)	
Golden State	.607	− 1.940	.231
	(1.93)	(3.38)	
Los Angeles Lakers	.188	− .938	.072
	(0.77)	(1.72)	
New York Knicks	.286	− .869	.095
	(1.20)	(1.99)	
Sacramento Kings	.333	− .564	.040
	(1.31)	(1.27)	

Table 8A.5 Ownership and Managerial Termination in Baseball

Club	Constant	Finish	Owner		R^2
			National League		
Atlanta	$-.777E-01$	$.833E-01$	Fuchs	$-.194E-01$	.116
	(0.53)	(3.13)		(0.83)	
			Perini	$.403E-01$	
				(1.23)	
			Turner	$.165E-01$	
				(0.59)	
Philadelphia	$.232E-01$	$.710E-01$	Baker	$.238E-02$	.108
	(0.18)	(2.79)		(0.11)	
			Carpenter	$-.163E-01$	
				(0.89)	
Chicago	$-.666E-01$	$.149$	W. Wrigley	$-.440E-01$	.210
	(0.61)	(4.70)		(1.27)	
			P. Wrigley	$-.722E-01$	
				(2.98)	
Pittsburgh	$-.296E-01$	$.750E-01$	Dreyfus	$-.457E-01$	.101
	(0.03)	(2.54)		(0.14)	
			Benswanger	$-.227E-01$	
				(0.58)	
			Galbreath	$-.231$	
				(0.81)	
Cincinnati	$-.902E-01$	$.102$	Crosley	$-.102E-01$	.208
	(0.88)	(4.56)		(0.53)	
St. Louis	$.108$	$.498E-01$	Busch	$-.174E-01$	.06
	(1.10)	(2.34)		(0.78)	
San Francisco	$-.317E-01$	$.845E-01$	C. Stoneham	$-.265E-01$	.12
	(0.40)	(3.22)		(0.76)	
			H. Stoneham	$-.211E-01$	
				(0.89)	

Table 8A.5 (*Continued*)

Club	Constant	Finish	Owner		R^2
			American League		
Baltimore	$-.268E-01$	$.708E-01$	Ball	$.708E-01$	.145
	(0.22)	(3.34)		(0.32)	
			Hoffberg	$-.315E-01$	
				(0.63)	
Detroit	$-.176$	$.118$	Briggs	$-.112$	.250
	(1.87)	(4.99)		(0.52)	
			Fetzer	$-.868E-01$	
				(0.35)	
Boston	$.681E-01$	$.667E-01$	Yawkey	$-.681E-02$	.103
	(0.66)	(3.05)		(0.35)	
Minnesota	$.504E-01$	$.828E-01$	Clark Griffith	$-.391E-01$	.123
	(0.42)	(3.35)		(1.77)	
			Cal Griffith	$-.223E-01$	
				(0.92)	
Chicago	$-.157$	$.113$	C. Comiskey	$.922E-02$	.231
	(1.42)	(4.07)		(0.41)	
			Comiskey family	$-.349E-01$	
				(1.53)	
New York	$.156E-01$	$.566E-01$	Ruppert	$.105E-01$	.274
	(0.19)	(2.73)		(0.35)	
			Webb-Topping	$.769E-01$	
				(1.00)	
			Steinbrenner	$.132$	
				(4.22)	
Oakland	$.117$	$.941E-02$	Finley	$.769E-01$	.263
	(1.44)	(0.61)		(4.84)	

Table 8A.6   Ownership and Improvement in Club Standing in Baseball

Club	Constant	Fired	Owner		R^2
National League					
Atlanta	.232	−.526	Fuchs	.294	.050
	(0.93)	(1.02)		(0.28)	
			Perini	−1.039	
				(1.17)	
			Turner	.294	
				(0.31)	
Philadelphia	.304	−.370	Baker	−3.08	.044
	(1.15)	(0.64)		(0.36)	
			Carpenter	−.933	
				(1.12)	
Chicago	.364	−.729	W. Wrigley	.492	.02
	(0.16)	(1.39)		(0.55)	
			P. Wrigley	.759	
				(1.17)	
Pittsburgh	.418	−1.420	Dreyfus	−.228E−14	.11
	(1.72)	(1.21)		(0.00)	
			Benswanger	−.155E−14	
				(0.00)	
			Galbreath	−.444	
				(0.34)	
Cincinnati	.488	−1.062	Crosley	−.108	.09
	(1.79)	(2.44)		(1.36)	
St. Louis	.317	−1.317	Busch	.571	.05
	(0.98)	(1.92)		(0.50)	
San Francisco	.169	−1.502	C. Stoneham	−5.667	.14
	(0.68)	(1.70)		(2.52)	
			H. Stoneham	1.033	
				(0.96)	

Table 8A.6 (*Continued*)

Club	Constant	Fired	Owner		R^2
			American League		
Baltimore	.183	−.883	Ball	.557	.039
	(0.67)	(1.60)		(0.59)	
			Hoffberg	−1.300	
				(0.59)	
Detroit	.446	−1.668	Briggs	.972E−01	.096
	(1.69)	(2.21)		(0.09)	
			Fetzer	.389	
				(0.35)	
Boston	.439	−1.203	Yawkey	−.210E−01	.067
	(1.50)	(1.97)		(0.03)	
Minnesota	.525	−1.900	Clark Griffith	.193	.095
	(1.64)	(2.06)		(0.17)	
			Cal Griffith	.575	
				(0.49)	
Chicago	.525	−1.650	C. Comiskey	.663	.125
	(2.02)	(2.16)		(0.73)	
			Comiskey family	−.708	
				(0.65)	
New York	.206	.169	Ruppert	−1.375	.046
	(0.79)	(0.22)		(1.09)	
			Webb-Topping	−1.042	
				(0.75)	
			Steinbrenner	−1.275	
				(1.30)	
Oakland	.123	−.568	Finley	−.556E−01	.016
	(0.47)	(0.75)		(0.06)	

Chapter One

1. *New York Times,* 11 April 1993, p. 23.

2. For forty-six of the eligible free agents in the NFL, average salary rose from $731,100 in 1992 to $2,037,300 in 1993, an increase of 178.7 percent. *New York Times,* 15 July 1993, p. B8.

3. Harold Seymour, *Baseball: The Early Years* (New York: Oxford University Press, 1960), 3–12. Seymour is the best source on the early history of baseball. I have been guided by his historical inquiry throughout the chapter.

4. Currently the minimum population rule in the American League is 2.4 million (waived if three-quarters of the clubs approve).

5. For an analysis of changes in baseball's playing rules and their effects on player performance and on scoring, see Gerald W. Scully, *The Business of Major League Baseball* (Chicago: University of Chicago Press, 1989), 51–74.

Not all rule changes have been player-driven. For example, until recent times great and deliberate differences existed among ball parks. The introduction of the "lively" ball and the banning of certain pitches (spitball and scuffball) in 1920 gave rise to power hitting. The Polo Grounds, with its short foul lines and deep center field, Ebbetts Field, with short power alleys, the Baker Bowl, with its very short right field fence, Yankee Stadium, built for Ruth's attributes, and other parks were built with particular characteristics of the player roster in mind. Minimum fence distances (introduced in 1959 for subsequent parks) have brought more uniformity to the playing fields as the old parks have disappeared. The huge cost (about $250 million for land, park, and infrastructure) of modern stadiums has promoted a multi-purpose design. The constraint that the stadium also serve as a football facility has led to a certain "cookie-cutter" uniformity to these stadiums. The new Camden Yards ballpark for the Baltimore Orioles is an exception.

6. U.S. House Committee of the Judiciary, *Organized Baseball,* Report of the Subcommittee on the Study of Monopoly Power, 82d Cong., 1st sess., 1952, H. Rept. 2002, 21.

7. James Quirk and Rodney D. Fort, *Pay Dirt: The Business of Professional Team Sports* (Princeton: Princeton University Press, 1992), 378–82.

8. U.S. Department of Commerce, Bureau of the Census, *Statistical Abstract of the United States, 1990* (Washington: GPO, 1990), 532.

9. In contrast, during the decade prior to the elimination of the reserve clause, the twenty-five-man roster cost was about 20–25 percent of club revenue. Today it is about 50 percent of revenue.

10. Scully, *Business,* 17.

11. Calculated from club salary data in Seymour, *Baseball,* 117.

12. U.S. House Committee on the Judiciary, Subcommittee on Study of Monopoly Power, *Study of Monopoly Power,* Pt. 6, *Organized Baseball.* Hearings. 82d Cong., 1st sess., 1952.

13. U.S. House, *Organized Baseball,* 6.

14. Quirk and Fort, *Pay Dirt,* 30.

15. Calculated from data in Quirk and Fort, *Pay Dirt,* 335.

16. Ibid., 33.

17. A rule or agreement is joint-wealth maximizing if in its presence the value of the n firms (teams) party to the rule rises. For example, the value of a franchise is greater under a reserve clause in the players' market because players earn less than their incremental contribution to team revenue. See Gerald W. Scully, "Pay and Performance in Major League Baseball," *American Economic Review* 64 (December 1974): 915–30. The monopsony rents associated with the restriction in the players' market increase the capitalized value of the franchises. For other examples of joint-wealth maximizing rules, see Scully, *Business,* and Brian L. Goff and Robert D. Tollison, *Sportometrics* (College Station: Texas A & M Press, 1990).

18. For a barrier to entry to exist in the Stiglerian sense, a cost must be imposed on the new firm that does not exist for the current firms in the industry. If there exists an exclusive contract between a publicly owned stadium and a team, entry of a rival team may be precluded. If access to a television contract is a necessary condition for the survival of a new league, and an exclusive contract is in force between the existing league and the television networks, the contract may be a barrier to entry. We will return to this problem later.

19. In baseball, National League clubs have territorial exclusivity within

10 miles of the city, while American League clubs have it within 100 miles. The existing club may reject location of a new club within its territory. Additionally, if the proposed entrant is to locate in a city of less than 2.4 million, three-quarters of the existing American League clubs must approve.

20. This is not to say that teams do not exploit the rules or move for changes in league rules that are favorable to their playing talents. Before the adoption of minimum fence distances in baseball, parks were built or modified to accommodate hitters or pitchers. Changes in the distance from the pitcher's mound to home plate, the strike zone, the introduction of the lively ball (1920), hash marks, the three-point rule, and so on all enhance relevant player skills and change the distribution of win-loss records among teams for a period of time. See Scully, *Business,* 63–74, for evidence of the effect of changes in the playing rules in baseball on the distribution of club win-loss records.

21. Scully, *Business,* 50–51.

22. Beyond the question of blocking the entry of a new league, the incentive for expansion is affected by the division of revenue among the existing teams. Until the advent of league contracts with network television, teams earned revenue from ticket sales and local broadcast contracts. Basketball and hockey have a 100–0 gate split, baseball overall about an 85–15 split, and football a 60–40 split. Network television contracts have grown in importance as a source of revenue, and they are divided equally among the teams. The more socialized the revenue, as in football, the weaker are the incentives to expand and the higher the compensation costs demanded by the existing teams, because a fixed or inelastic increase in revenues has to be divided over a larger number of teams. The $95 million price for the 1993 expansion franchises in baseball reflects the attempt of existing franchises to obtain compensation for reduced shares of the network television contract. See Scully, *Business,* 146–47.

23. The existence of monopoly rents has given rise to the entry of rival leagues in all of the sports. On the whole, rival leagues have not endured, partly because of the predatory practices of the existing leagues. It takes considerable time to be credible on the playing field. That credibility is essential in building a loyal fan following. While the credibility is being built, rival leagues generally are operated at a financial loss. Losses can be sustained only for so long before the owner's wealth is eaten away.

24. Scully, *Business,* 85–97.

25. The assertion that teams face the same incremental cost function is not extreme. Certainly there are other costs incurred in providing games, but there is no reason to believe and not much empirical evidence that the supply functions of these inputs and services differ across teams.

26. See Scully, *Business,* 75–97.

27. In baseball broadcast fees were $783,000 per team in 1960. By the mid-1970s broadcast fees averaged less than 25 percent of club revenues. Now broadcast fees are about 40 percent of club revenues in baseball and a higher fraction in football. See Scully, *Business,* 108, 118.

28. The relationship between market size and win percent and club attendance or revenues is well known. See Scully, "Pay and Performance."

29. There is no denying that owners may have different motives other than the profitability of the club. At a time when ownership of a club was the sole source of income for the owner, the altruistic motive to "win at any price" was not sustainable, because it meant a loss of wealth. In more modern times ownership of clubs may be a strategy to improve net income in other lines of business. August Busch bought the St. Louis Cardinals to increase beer sales. Some teams (e.g., Chicago, Atlanta) are owned by broadcast interests and are an important part of programming. The bottom line on the balance sheet of the clubs owned for these purposes may be of secondary importance to larger corporate interests. See Scully, *Business,* 129–44.

30. The New York Yankees cable television deal at roughly $50 million per year has exacerbated the dispersion in revenues from the sale of local broadcast rights. Some clubs in small broadcast markets like Seattle, Cleveland, or Kansas City earn only $3 million or so. Teams in Los Angeles or in other large markets earn two or three times that amount.

31. Ira Horowitz, "Sports Broadcasting," in *Government and the Sports Business,* ed. Roger G. Noll (Washington, D.C.: The Brookings Institution, 1974).

32. Prior to the early 1950s (the rise of television), actors were "reserved" by movie studies. An actor could be loaned out to another studio for a picture, but the fee went to the studio that owned his or her contract. Actors were not free to sell their talents to anyone making films.

33. Ray Kennedy and Nancy Williamson, "Money: The Monster Threatening Sports," *Sports Illustrated* (17 July 1978): 46.

34. On the motives, see Simon Rottenberg, "The Baseball Players' Labor Market," *Journal of Political Economy* 64 (June 1956): 242–58, and Mohamed El-Hodiri and James Quirk, "An Economic Model of a Professional Sports League," *Journal of Political Economy* 79 (December 1971): 1302–19. On the evidence, see Scully, *Business,* 93–97.

35. That the ownership of the property right (contract) does not affect the allocation of resources but does affect income distribution is known as the Coase theorem. See Ronald H. Coase, "The Problem of Social Cost," *Journal of Law and Economics* 3 (October 1960): 1–44.

36. Scully, *Business,* 65–70.

37. Scully, *Business,* 152.

Chapter Two

1. For example, see D. N. MacDonald and M. O. Reynolds, "Are Baseball Players Paid Their Marginal Revenue Products?" Unpublished ms. (Texas A & M University, June, 1989).

2. G. S. Becker and G. J. Stigler, "Law Enforcement and Compensation of Enforcers," *Journal of Legal Studies* 3 (1974): 1–18.

3. E. Lazear, "Why Is There Mandatory Retirement?" *Journal of Political Economy* 87 (1979): 1261–84; E. Lazear, "Agency, Earnings Profiles, Productivity, and Hours Restrictions," *American Economic Review* 71 (1981): 606–20.

4. E. Lazear and S. Rosen, "Rank-order Tournaments as Optimum Labor Contracts," *Journal of Political Economy* 89 (1981): 841–64.

5. Define team j's performance, Q_j, as a function of the talent, t_i, of the N individual players on the club, plus a random (luck) component, ϵ_j, according to $Q_j = T_j + \epsilon_j$, for $T_j = T(t_{ji})$, and $i = 1, N$, where ϵ_j are i.i.d. (normally distributed) and $E(\epsilon) = 0$.

The probability that club j will defeat club k, W_{jk}, in a randomly scheduled contest is

$$W_{jk} = \text{prob}(Q_j > Q_k) = \text{prob}(T_j - T_k > \epsilon_k - \epsilon_j)$$
$$\equiv F(T_j - T_k),$$

where $E(\epsilon_k - \epsilon_j) = 0$, and F is the cdf (cumulative density function) of $\epsilon_k - \epsilon_j$.

6. If league revenues are determined by league-wide talent levels, $B(\Sigma T_j)$, revenues per club are $\overline{B}_j = B(\Sigma T_j)/J$. Local revenues for a team are determined by expected team performance, $L_j(W_{jk})$; expected team revenue per contest is thus $ER_j = \overline{B}_j + L_j(W_{jk})$.

7. Player i's performance, q_i, in a rank-order tournament for the starting position is determined by his athletic endowment and enhanced by investment in playing skill, t_i, plus exogenous factors that affect performance stochastically, e_i, as in $q_i = t_i + e_i$.

Let p_{12} be the probability that player 1 will outperform player 2 in a random pairing for a contest and obtain the starting position. Then

$$p_{12} = \text{prob}(q_1 > q_2) = \text{prob}(t_1 - t_2 > e_2 - e_1)$$
$$\equiv D(t_1 - t_2),$$

where $E(e_2 - e_1) = 0$, and D is the cdf of $e_2 - e_1$.

8. $ES_1 = p_{12}S_1 + (1 - p_{12})S_2$, and $ES_2 = (1 - p_{12})S_1 + p_{12}S_2$.

9. G. W. Scully, "Pay and Performance in Major League Baseball," *American Economic Review* 64 (December, 1974): 915–30.

10. A considerable portion of the salary data utilized here for the earlier periods came from Rodney Fort (baseball) and Roger Noll (basketball). I am grateful to them for providing their data.

11. M. El-Hodiri and J. Quirk, "An Economic Model of a Professional Sports League," *Journal of Political Economy* 79 (November/December, 1971): 1302–19.

12. The lower bound on the critical value (95 percent) of the *F*-tests holds if the smaller sample is utilized.

13. The link between team performance and team wins, and between wins and club revenue is known. The link between player performance and club revenue is also established. Transformation of the production measure (TOTBASES) to a revenue measure (marginal revenue product of performance) will leave the index unaffected, because what is in the numerator is also in the denominator.

Chapter Three

1. Another source of measurement error arises from the method by which the winner is determined. In golf it is the player with the lowest score. Although officials make rulings on out-of-bounds, whether the ball may be moved, and so on, judging plays a trivial role in determining the winner. In tennis, judging is more important to the outcome of a match as the spread in talent narrows. Bashing and intimidation of the judges is notorious by some players and may have high value when the margin between the players in the match is small. In sports like amateur boxing, ice skating, and diving, judging adds a lot of noise to the correlation between performance and rank-order of finish.

2. Lavoie and Grenier find that penalty minutes per game, which is a proxy for rough play, is a significant and relatively large covariate of pay for forwards. Marc Lavoie and Gilles Grenier, "Discrimination and Salary Determination in the National Hockey League: 1977 and 1989 Compared," in G. W. Scully, ed., *Advances in the Economics of Sport* (Greenwich, Conn.: JAI Press, 1992), 151–75.

3. David N. Leband, "How the Structure of Competition Influences Performance in Professional Sports: The Case of Tennis and Golf," in B. L. Goff and R. D. Tollison, eds., *Sportometrics* (College Station: Texas A & M University Press, 1990), 138–39.

4. James Quirk and Rodney D. Fort have used this formulation in assessing the effect of the revenue-sharing rule on the distribution of playing talent within a league. James Quirk and Rodney D. Fort, *Pay Dirt: The Business of Professional Team Sports* (Princeton: Princeton University Press, 1992), 273–75.

5. Gerald W. Scully, "Pay and Performance in Major League Baseball," *American Economic Review* 64 (December 1974): 915–30.

6. Newspapers and sports magazines now publish player salaries in team sports on a regular basis. The data are from these standard sources. Data on the earnings in the individual sports and auto racing are from the various associations.

7. The values (and standard errors) of the Lorenz ordinates for the first four independent quintiles, L_i, were estimated (not presented here). The relevant statistic is

$$T_i = (L_i^a - L_i^b)/[(SE_i^a)^2/N_a + (SE_i^b)^2/N_b]^{1/2}, i = 1,2,3,4.$$

T_i follows the Student maximum modulus distribution.

The test for Lorenz dominance follows John A. Bishop, J. P. Formby, and W. J. Smith, "Lorenz Dominance and Welfare: Changes in the U.S. Distribution of Income, 1967–1986," *The Review of Economics and Statistics* 73 (Feb. 1991): 134–39. The measure of distribution-free standard errors for Lorenz ordinates, SE_i, is given by C. M. Beach and R. Davidson, "Distribution-Free Statistical Inference with Lorenz Curves and Income Shares," *Review of Economic Studies* 50 (Oct. 1983): 723–35.

Lorenz dominance occurs if there is at least one positive and significant T value in the independent quintiles and no negative and significant values. The critical value for T at the 5 percent level is 3.93. Two distributions are considered equivalent if there are no significant values of T. They cannot be rank-compared if there are both positive and significant and negative and significant values of T.

8. Rodney Fort provided the baseball salary data for 1973 and the mean salary data (1970–74) and Gini coefficients (1968–72, 1974, 1986–88) for some of the years. Rodney Fort, "A Pay and Performance Omnibus: Is the Field of Dreams Barren?", a paper prepared for a Middlebury College Conference, April 5–6, 1991.

There were 223 observations of baseball-player salaries for 1973. Since players and owners use the newspapers to negotiate salaries, salary data in baseball is the richest of the sports. Nevertheless rookies are under-represented. I compared the 1973 sample with the 1990 population based on the distribution of years in the majors. The 1973 sample was not far off. I added 7 rookie salaries to match the distributions. Thus, my sample size is 230 observations.

9. Roger Noll provided an economics honors paper that he supervised on basketball (Kim Akers, "Overpaid Boys or Underpaid Men: The Salary Determination Process in the NBA," Economics Honors Thesis, Stanford University, June 3, 1991). Sample salary data are available from 1967–68 to 1969–70, 1972–73 to 1974–75, 1978–79 to 1980–81, and 1983–84 to 1987–88. Generally, the sample is biased toward the journeymen and star players. The 1967–68 sample was especially good. The data on nine teams

covered 75 percent of the roster. There were some missing observations of notables (e.g., Wilt Chamberlain, Bill Russell, Elgin Baylor), but mostly rookie salaries were missing. I used data from my own files and educated guesses on the salaries of the missing players. I added 28 observations to the available 84 observations. The Gini on the Akers data was .247 compared to a Gini of .274 for my expanded sample. I believe mine is a more accurate description of the distribution, because the sample is the population for nine of twelve teams. In figure 3.4 I used her salary data to calculate Gini coefficients. They are biased downward because rookies and journeymen players are under-represented; nevertheless, they are informative with respect to trend. Note that the Ginis for 1967–68 and 1988–89, which are based on the population of players, can be taken as definitive.

10. Salary inequality continues to rise in baseball. The Gini coefficient was .54 for the 1991 season.

11. Quirk and Fort, *Pay Dirt,* 238.

12. The measure is the slugging average multiplied by the number of times at bat plus bases on balls plus stolen bases. Clearly, players do more than bat, but as a single metric of player quality, the measure is unsurpassed. Obviously, total bases are highly correlated with runs scored. Winning in baseball means producing more runs than the opponent. Measuring pitching performance as a single metric is more problematical. Undoubtedly the objective of pitching is to minimize opponent runs. Games won, innings pitched, ERA, and other measures are common standards of pitching performance, but each fails to capture pitching performance in a single dimension. For example, ERA does not take innings pitched into account, and vice versa. Total earned runs may be higher for a great pitcher who works regularly in the rotation than a weaker pitcher who appears less frequently. For these reasons the distribution of pitching performance is not examined.

13. Effort in team sports is uniform across players, because all compete (or are available) in an equal number of fixed, scheduled contests. Among players in the individual sports, there is no control for effort. The data are on annual earnings, with each player competing in various numbers of tournaments. Thus there is a compounding of the return to performance and the return to effort. It is assumed that there is a positively sloped supply of effort, so that the more talented players enter the most (or at least the most rewarding) tournaments.

Chapter Four

1. Gerald W. Scully, *The Business of Major League Baseball* (Chicago: University of Chicago Press, 1989), 85–93.

2. James Quirk and Rodney D. Fort, *Pay Dirt: The Business of Professional Team Sports* (Princeton: Princeton University Press, 1992): 240–68.

3. See Scully, *Business,* 75–80, and Quirk and Fort, *Pay Dirt,* 271–79 for further details.

4. Quirk and Fort, *Pay Dirt,* 247.

5. None of the statistical results presented in the appendix tables are sensitive to the choice of the length of the moving average. All of the equations were estimated with the raw data and with moving averages longer than three years. The pattern in the signs of the autoregressive terms was not particularly affected by the choice of the length of the moving average. On empirical grounds, the three-year moving average was superior.

6. While there is evidence that the DW test is reasonably powerful against higher-order autoregression, it is known that lagged values of the dependent variable bias the test toward a finding of an absence of serial correlation. As a cross-check, all of the results were subjected to general LM tests. In all cases the findings were an absence of serial correlation from the residuals of the Box-Jenkins equations. See R. C. Blattberg, "Evaluation of the Power of the Durbin-Watson Statistic for Non-First-Order Serial Correlation Alternatives," *Review of Economics and Statistics* 55 (August 1973): 508–15.

Chapter Five

1. *Financial World,* 9 July 1991.

2. Readers willing to accept my characterization of the effect of reputation on the sale of firms may skip the next section.

3. George A. Akerlof, "The Market for 'Lemons': Quality Uncertainty and the Market Mechanism," *Quarterly Journal of Economics* 84 (1970): 488–500. Benjamin Klein and Kenneth B. Leffler, "The Role of Market Forces in Assuring Contractual Performance," *Journal of Political Economy* 79 (1971): 1302–19.

4. Cheating on product quality or fraud in a market with asymmetry of information between supplier and customer is not considered here. See Michael R. Darby and Edi Karni, "Free Competition and the Optimal Amount of Fraud," *Journal of Law and Economics* 16 (April 1973): 67–88.

5. Lee P. Strobel, *Reckless Homicide? Ford's Pinto Trial* (South Bend, Ind.: And Books, 1980), 40–41.

6. David A. Aaker, "Guarding the Power of a Brand Name," *New York Times* 30 November 1991, p. F 13.

7. The *t*-value of the coefficient of the team slugging average on the team win percent was 3.88; the *t*-value for the team ERA was 7.81.

8. Roger G. Noll, "Attendance and Price Setting," in Noll, ed., *Government and the Sports Business* (Washington: The Brookings Institution, 1974), 115–57.

9. Gerald W. Scully, *The Business of Major League Baseball* (Chicago: University of Chicago Press, 1989), 101–16.

10. Mohamed El-Hodiri and James Quirk, "An Economic Model of a Professional Sports League," *Journal of Political Economy* 79 (1971): 1302–19. Philip K. Porter, "Market Advantage as Rent: Do Professional Teams in Larger Markets Have a Competitive Advantage?" In G. W. Scully, ed., *Advances in the Economics of Sport*, vol. 1 (Greenwich, Conn.: JAI Press, 1992).

11. The *t*-value is 5.88.

12. Henry G. Manne, "Mergers and the Market for Corporate Control," *Journal of Political Economy* 73 (April 1965): 110–20.

13. James Cassing and Richard W. Douglas, "Implications of the Auction Mechanism in Baseball's Free Agent Draft." *Southern Economic Journal* 47 (July 1980): 110–21.

14. *New York Times*, 2 November 1991, pp. 19, 21.

15. Data on franchise sales of clubs over their history have been collected by James Quirk and Rodney D. Fort, *Pay Dirt: The Business of Professional Team Sports* (Princeton: Princeton University Press, 1992), and are utilized here. A sale is defined as the transfer of a franchise to a new owner, either in its entirety or in substantial part. Transfers to spouses and children at the time of the owner's death are not considered sales.

16. The log likelihood converged at four iterations for both models. The χ^2 for the logit model with two degrees of freedom was 59.45, and for the probit it was 59.08, with both Prob $> \chi^2 = .00005$ percent.

Chapter Six

1. Early data on the profitability of team sports are given by Roger G. Noll, "The U.S. Team Sports Industry: An Introduction," in R. G. Noll, ed., *Government and the Sports Business* (Washington: The Brookings Institution, 1974), 1–32. For more current evidence of club profits in baseball see Gerald W. Scully, *The Business of Major League Baseball* (Chicago: University of Chicago Press, 1989), 117–44.

2. A. Baldo et al., "Secrets of the Front Office," *Financial World*, 9 July 1991, pp. 28–43; Michael K. Ozanian and Stephen Taub, "Big Leagues, Bad Business," *Financial World*, 7 July 1992, pp. 34–51.

3. For sports-accounting issues as they relate to major league baseball, see Scully, *Business*, 129–44.

4. James Quirk and Rodney D. Fort, *Pay Dirt: The Business of Professional Team Sports* (Princeton: Princeton University Press, 1992), 49–63; 377–78.

5. I have indicated that one should be cautious in using estimated values for the franchises in 1991. Recent (1992) sale prices (e.g., Houston Astros,

San Francisco Giants) are close to the estimated values of the clubs; nevertheless, an estimate is not an exchange price. I took the latest exchange price for the franchise (cases = 45) and calculated the internal rate of return between the early exchange price and the most current exchange price. A correlation of those internal rates of return with the internal rates of return in table 6.1 yielded a value of .67, which is significant at the 99 percent level. I conclude that the estimates have some value.

6. Florence Setzer and Jonathan Levy, *Broadcast Television in a Multichannel Marketplace,* OPP Working Paper No: 26, Office of Plans and Policy (Washington: Federal Communications Commission, June, 1991), 36.

7. Eliot Jones, *The Trust Problem in the United States* (New York: Macmillan, 1921).

8. U.S. Department of Commerce, *Historical Statistics of the United States,* Series V 285–305, 941.

9. Setzer and Levy, *Broadcast Television,* 36.

10. Ibid., 40.

11. Ibid., 41.

12. Ibid., 34.

13. Ibid., 36, 39.

14. Data on franchise prices over the history of the franchises and number of sales (years in which sales or partial sales took place) have been collected by James Quirk and Rodney D. Fort (see note 4). These data tend to come from published accounts and are subject to error. The data were used to determine the length of tenure of ownership in the survival analysis below. Because sales of franchises are often partial, the definition of a sale employed here is useful. All internal transactions due to an owner's death (team or partial assets to the spouse or children) were not treated as sales unless the assets were then sold to third parties. Small asset transfers and accumulations of assets over time to obtain larger blocks of the assets by a majority owner also were ignored. Thus a sale is the transfer of the entire team assets or of a substantial block of those assets to another party. According to this definition of a sale, there were 387 sales in the four sports.

15. B. A. Okner, "Taxation and Sports Enterprises," in Roger G. Noll, ed., *Government and the Sports Business* (Washington: The Brookings Institution, 1974), 159–83; Quirk and Fort, *Pay Dirt,* 121.

16. The log-likelihood function converged after three iterations at -1466.5. The χ^2 statistic is the likelihood-ratio test that the coefficients are zero. The χ^2 statistic has two degrees of freedom and a value of 6.75 with Prob $> \chi^2 = .0342$ percent. We accept that these are significant covariates of the hazard rate.

17. The asymptotic t-value was 1.49, with an asymptotic significance level of .137 percent.

18. The asymptotic t-value was 1.66, with an asymptotic significance level of .097 percent.

Chapter Seven

1. Gerald W. Scully, *The Business of Major League Baseball* (Chicago: University of Chicago Press, 1989), 140–43.

2. The simple production process may be stochastic, rather than deterministic. In this case W is replaced with its density function and associated cumulative distribution function: $f(W|e, \psi)$ and $F(W|e, \psi)$. Higher levels of coaching effort decrease the probability that the smaller levels of output will be realized. That is, $F_e(W|e, \psi) \le 0$. In the case of stochastic production, the ratio e/e^* only partly measures managerial effort or efficiency. Part of the lost output may be due to random factors beyond the agent's control.

3. The residuals from the regressions estimated on the basis of equation (7.2) were examined, and no pattern related to trend was found. Several tests were performed on the residuals (e.g., the squared residuals against trend) with no significant results.

4. Technically, the condition is $S_{max} = \Sigma_{ij} (\partial S/\partial X_i)X_i + (\partial S/\partial X_j)X_j$, $i = 1, n; j = 1, m$; and, $i \ne j$.

5. Technically, the condition is $OS_{min} = \Sigma_{ij} (\partial OS/\partial Y_i)Y_i + (\partial OS/\partial Y_j)Y_j$.

6. The choice of the estimation procedure for the production (win) function in equation (7.2) depends on the assumption made regarding the error term, ε. Three specifications were employed here: the deterministic frontier function, the stochastic frontier function, and the maximum-likelihood Gamma frontier function.

The deterministic frontier function is estimated by minimizing the sum of the absolute residuals. Therefore this approach considers all deviations from the efficient, frontier function as arising from inefficiency. A criticism is that only part of the error term may be deterministic; part may be truly stochastic. The error term may be of the form $\varepsilon = u + v$, where u is a one-sided disturbance term representing the degree of managerial inefficiency, and v is a symmetric, normally distributed random influence. In the case of the win production function, the random component would be luck; some games are won and some are lost, not for reasons of relative playing skill or coaching ability, but for reasons of referee error or other events beyond the control of the contestants. Two stochastic frontier functions were estimated: one with a normally distributed error term, v, and the other with the error term assumed to be Gamma-distributed. Neither of these specifications were superior to the deterministic frontier estimates. Therefore only the latter are presented here.

7. The data for baseball are from 1876 to 1989 and are contained in *The*

Baseball Encyclopedia, 8th ed. (New York: Macmillan, 1990). All teams and leagues were included except for the Union Association teams in the 1884 season. Too many teams folded too early in that league to make their inclusion valid. The data for basketball are from David S. Neft and Richard M. Cohen, *The Sports Encyclopedia: Pro Basketball*, 3d ed. (New York: St. Martin's Press, 1990), and cover all leagues and teams from the 1937–38 season to the 1989–90 season. The data for football are from 1933 to 1989 and for all leagues and teams. Prior to the 1960 season, the data is from *Official 1985 National Football League Record and Fact Book;* for the period 1960–89, the data are from Neft and Cohen, *The Sports Encyclopedia: Pro Football*, 8th ed. (New York: St. Martin's Press, 1990). The head coach list prior to 1960 was obtained from the *Pro Football Guide*, 1990 edition (St. Louis: The Sporting News, 1990).

8. The data record in all of the sports, especially for baseball, covers a very substantial period of time. Despite the theoretical arguments about constant variance over time, in light of substantial rule changes, innovation, the allocation of drafting rights, free agency or reduced restrictions in player-initiated movement, and the number of contests, one might be suspicious about combining data from the early period of the sport with data from its more mature period. As a cross-check, I divided the data in baseball into the period 1876–1900 and 1901–89. Except for the introduction of the lively ball in 1920 and occasional changes in the strike zone, the vast majority of rule changes had taken place by the end of the National League–American League War. The coefficient of ln (S/OS) on ln W was .9493 for the period 1876–1900 and .9430 for 1901–89. The coefficients are the same by the standard statistical test. In football the division was 1933–1966 and 1967–89. The coefficients were 1.3363 and 1.3694 and were not different from one another statistically. Similar results were obtained for basketball.

9. Philip K. Porter and Gerald W. Scully, "Measuring Managerial Efficiency: The Case of Baseball," *Southern Economic Journal* (January 1982): 642–50.

10. A t-test on the difference in the means yielded $t = 4.60$.

11. The t-value was 0.05 on the difference between the means.

12. Porter and Scully, "Measuring Managerial Efficiency."

Chapter Eight

1. Serial correlation is a possibility in time series analysis, although unlikely with a binary dependent variable. Durbin-Watson statistics were obtained, but all indicated an absence of serial correlation and hence are not reported.

△

△

△ **INDEX**

▼

▼